Life Is a Stamp Collection

from child traveler to flight attendant

M. Angela Sanders

Simon Publishing LLC

Copyright © 2021 M. Angela Sanders

Cover design © 2021 Joanne Simon Tailele

Simon Publishing LLC ® is a registered trademark.

Published by Simon Publishing LLC

www.SimonPublishingLLC.com

All rights reserved. No part of this may be reproduced in any forms or by any electronic or mechanical means including information storage and retrieval systems—except in the case of brief quotations, embodied in critical articles or reviews—without permission in writing from its publisher, Simon Publishing LLC.

This is a memoir. Any persons, living or dead, or places are seen through the lens of the author and the author's memory.

All brand names and product names used in this book are trademarks, registered trademarks, or trade names of their respective holders. Simon Publishing LLC is not associated with any product or vendor in this book.

Library of Congress Control Number: 2021920998

ISBN: 97817376246-0-8 – Trade Paperback

ISBN: 97817376246-1-5 – Hard Cover

ISBN: 978173762466-2-2 – e-Book

20210824123

Life Is a Stamp Collection

from child traveler to flight attendant

M. Angela Sanders

M. Angela Sanders

Dedication

I dedicate this book to Dr. Leon Hesser and his family!

He and his wife, Florence, were very encouraging regarding my putting down my humble but adventuresome journeys in this book.

In their lives, while enduring hardships living outside of our wonderful USA, they, along with their son, George, and daughter, Gwen, selflessly worked to end food shortages in Pakistan and Bangladesh.

Florence and Gwen are now deceased, but they left marks as blessings on many hearts — including mine — as they traveled through this lifetime.

Acknowledgments

I acknowledge and thank my sister, Brenda, and my brothers, Craig and Roger, for the bonds that kept us going forward even when we were dropped off in various countries to learn the different customs and pretend we were not afraid.

We were not to show our fear or weakness or discontent. So, we displayed the British custom of "stiff upper lip," and we were expanded into capable children who adjusted with courage and denied our fears.

I do appreciate our Scottish grandparents, Silas Ervin Craig and Pearlee Stanley Craig, who were part of the covered wagon era, arriving as young babies to the new state of Arkansas. They were always very generous with their love, not only to their family but to others who had less. If my grandfather saw a child without a winter coat or shoes, he would take the child and buy them whatever they needed.

This was the foundation for his family's values, which were passed down through our generations.

M. Angela Sanders
Table of Contents

Dedication... iv
Acknowledgments.. v
Foreword viii
Chapter One
    Little Blonde Girl in Nepal... 1
    Lucknow.. 3
    Kathmandu, Nepal... 5
    Current Day Nepal... 13
Chapter Two
    How we ended up in Nepal... 16
    What it was like in Nepal.. 20
Chapter Three
    Climbing Mount Everest... 22
    Sir Edmund Hillary's Devastating Loss.. 26
    The Fabulous Flemings... 27
    Church Fellowship... 30
    History of Himalayas and Kashmir... 32
    The Nepalese Government.. 35
    Preparing to Leave Nepal.. 37
Chapter Four
    Growing Up in Historical Simla, India.. 39
    American boarding school – Woodstock.. 54
Chapter Five
    High School and College in Arkansas... 57
Chapter Six
    Walking Across Oceans... 66
    High Heels, Girdles and Gloves... 66
    Visiting Parents in Thailand... 69
    Bill Cherry and Eddie Rickenbacker... 73
Chapter Seven
    My Marriage to Dr. Al Edinger... 75
    Inside the Iron Curtain.. 84
    Father retired from Foreign Service... 87
    The Watergate Trial.. 89
Chapter Eight
    Farrokh of Iran.. 92
    The Golden Cage.. 98
    Dissolved Marriage.. 102
    The Right Reverend Monsignor... 104
Chapter Nine
    Peru 107
    Mexico.. 111
    Punta Bandera and Donald Trump... 113

Chapter Ten
    Michener/ Caravans/Afghanistan 115
    Kenya, Africa 121
Chapter Eleven
    That PSA Flight 125
Chapter Twelve
    A Holiday Trip through Russia 128
    Stalin's Only Daughter 135
Chapter Thirteen
    A Flight Attendant's Worst Nightmare 137
Chapter Fourteen
    Layover Cities 140
    Casablanca 140
    Charles Lindbergh 141
    Honolulu 142
Chapter Fifteen
    Michael Summers 143
    Savoring Egypt's History 144
Chapter Sixteen
    Father's Close Call 149
    Revisit to Ellerslie Villa 151
    Health Concerns 151
    Ruptured Appendix in Japan 152
Chapter Seventeen
    At Home on Marco Island 161
    The Terrifying 9/11 Disaster 161
    Philosophers' Café 163
    The Forester My Father Trusted 168
    Guardian Ad Litem Volunteer 170
Chapter Eighteen
    Back to India after 60 years 172
    Goodbye to American Airlines 174
Chapter Nineteen
    A Day on Capitol Hill with Senator Bill and Grace Nelson 175
    "Welcome to Florida" Women's International Club 176
    Rummikub 178
Epilogue: Reflections 179

Foreword

Angela Sanders, one of the brightest individuals whom I have known in my entire career, is also exceptionally friendly – and beautiful -- it's no surprise that she had a fascinating forty-year career as an airline stewardess. And her childhood experience, much of which was spent growing up in then-primitive Nepal and neighboring India, was interesting indeed.

But one of the many reasons that I was fascinated by her story was that her parents had taken her, as a ten-year-old child, and her younger siblings in 1952 to the Asian subcontinent where her father would help increase food production in Nepal and later in India. He had been doing that in Arkansas for a number of years, so when he learned of President Harry Truman's Point Four Program to help poorer countries in the world increase their food production, he volunteered.

Angela's father, Everette Sanders, was part of the first wave of Foreign Service Technical Assistance Officers to go to this Hindu/Buddhist nation under President Truman's Point Four Program. The mission was to help relieve hunger and poverty in this nation of mostly impoverished people. Nepal did not yet have an American Embassy; the Point Four team constituted the American Embassy.

Let me explain briefly why I was particularly interested in Mr. Sanders' job in Nepal and later in India. That is almost exactly the kind of work that I had done during my career in International Agricultural Development, starting initially in Pakistan in 1966. When Pakistan was offered as an assignment, I jumped at the chance. My team of a dozen American agricultural advisors and I helped introduce Norman Borlaug's wheat technology which doubled wheat production in Pakistan in four years and relieved hunger and malnutrition. Essentially the same thing happened in India, for which Dr. Borlaug was awarded the Nobel Peace Prize in 1970. In 2006, I wrote his biography, ***The Man Who Fed the World.***

Shortly after the book was published, Angela Sanders, who then lived fairly near us in Florida invited my wife, Florence, and me to her house to discuss the Borlaug biography and some of the many things that were similar in nature which each of us had been involved in during our careers. We encouraged her to write her fascinating story.

When I started receiving elements of the story, I was ecstatic. What a delight! Angela describes well her career as an American Airlines Stewardess.

She was, and IS, one of the most beautiful stewardesses that I had ever seen in my many flights to distant countries. And you probably have already guessed that she had a series of romances!

In this memoir, she includes pictures and describes some of her first-hand meetings with many noteworthy people. Among these were Sir Edmond Hillary, the first person to summit Nepal's Mount Everest, the highest mountain on Earth; and the king and other members of the royal family in Nepal; and she describes having visited a number of international places and events.

The stories she tells in *Life is a Stamp Collection, from child traveler to life as a flight attendant* are delightful.

I am sure you will agree.   Leon Hesser

M. Angela Sanders

Chapter One

Little Blonde Girl in Nepal

As a ten-year-old blue-eyed and blonde girl from Arkansas, I discovered life is a stamp collection when my family and I were suddenly transplanted inside Nepal in early 1952. It was in the time of the boll weevil in Arkansas, and DDT was sprayed airily on cotton and soybean crops. A song was even written about the Boll Weevil, and I can still hear it in my memory. This would set the tone of my adventures for the next fifty years.

After driving from Arkansas to Washington, DC, and seeing historical sites along the route, we rented an apartment on Layfette Circle. We lived here for about two months while Daddy went through indoctrination.

Then the time came for us to fly to India with stopovers in Paris and Beirut. When we finally landed at the New Delhi Airport, a bus was there to take us to our hotel. The sights on the roads to our hotel must have really frightened my parents, as they became so protective, they prohibited us from going places where other foreign children were permitted.

We waited and waited some more for Daddy to be notified of his assignment. Of course, we kids were confined inside the Ambassador Hotel. We could not go outside and play in the yards. The heat would be unbearable even for this little ten-year-old blonde girl who had lived in the hot, lazy-day breezes of Arkansas, among the lightning bugs and beautiful rivers, creeks, and hills.

As days turned into weeks, I fancied I was Robin Hood. I talked the other American kids into being my followers and led them through treacherous "tunnels." When it was time to go back to our rooms and clean up for a meal, we did, so our parents wouldn't know we had been exploring places they would not have approved of—complete with rats!

From our hotel windows, we watched the *malis*, the yard keepers, who tilted their goat-belly bags and let the water fall gently from one end of the skin onto the flowers. Sheep grazed the grass which tended to the "mowing."

We soon discovered the horrific conditions of the poor, forgotten street people. They and the beggars were known as the "untouchables." They were called *dalits*.

Though labeling under the caste system had been banned a few years before under Mahatma Gandhi's direction, discrimination remained evident. Gandhi's edict that women no longer had to walk two paces behind their husbands fared maybe a bit better.

On the outside porches *wallas*, sellers, sold from their rather dirty bags of jewelry and colorful stones. Daddy bought us all stones, which would not be put into mountings until my parents were based in Bangkok in the mid-1960s. My amethyst turned out to be fake, but I still wear it from time to time.

One day Daddy took us into the lobby because the American Ambassador to India was there with his wife and one daughter. At that time, I had not a clue exactly what an ambassador was, but I knew he must be most important as Americans were chatting around him.

Many years later, I would be given the book, *Many Promises to Keep*, written by Ambassador Bowles. From it, I learned more about his life's adventures.

Now here in 1952 in Delhi I was seeing him! His daughter was holding a white poodle. In the States, I had a little black Scottie dog, but I had never seen a French poodle.

In 1951, Chester Bowles had volunteered to President

Harry Truman to be the Ambassador to India. When President Truman asked him why in the world would he want to go to India, Mr. Bowles, a Democrat, said, "There is an opportunity to help move India more toward democracy."

One morning for breakfast there was an offering of shredded wheat, which had been one of my favorite things in the States. One thing I noticed was that there was not a mutton offering at all, as there had been on every other meal choice previously. There must have been a steady supply of mutton; whenever one looked out upon the hotel's green lawn sheep would be grazing to keep the grass at a certain level.

While outside sightseeing, bicycle bells rang constantly, letting all know that they must scurry out of the way. Horse-drawn jitneys, with enough room for four people, jostled the passengers forward, the driver shouting, "*Jai hey, jai hey!*" to all to get out of the way immediately.

While there, I discovered hot cashew nuts warmed in oil and lightly salted. It is still such a fond memory!

Finally, after boredom set in and having explored both Old and New Delhi, our family was shifted to Lucknow, as a change of scenery from New Delhi, while waiting for our final assignment.

Lucknow

Shortly after we arrived in Lucknow in late summer, the Nepalese Government and King Tribhuvan worked out the details for a technical assistance program with officials of President Truman's Point Four Program. Daddy was asked if he would be interested in going to Kathmandu instead of being posted in India. He was.

So, it turned out we would be going to Kathmandu, Nepal, and not staying in India! But for now, we would be in Lucknow, where I was introduced to the world of stamp collecting.

As there was nothing to keep us occupied, one day we went to the bazaar to a place which sold stamps and albums. I purchased an album which was a bit soiled on the front, but that was just minor to me, as the stamps to be put into the spaces inside were beautiful and would help my world of adventuresome dreams. Apparently, I did not know that I was already in an adventure. This was a whole new world, nurtured by this new album.

Roger, my youngest brother, got through those rather boring days in Lucknow by giving his new caged parrot a bath every few hours until finally the bird was found "claws heavenward." It seems that a bird can only be baptized, a-la-Baptist-style, so many times until its maker must step in and call the forlorn critter home.

I learned that Lucknow was a historical location. Gandhi and his followers had done much of their planning there for the non-violent overthrow of the British. *Gandhiji* (*Ji* is a Hindi title of respect) and Nehru met for the first time in Lucknow at the time of the Lucknow Congress during the Christmas of 1916. Nehru writes that Gandhi seemed very distant, different, and as political as were many of the young men of that time. Jawaharlal

Nehru regrouped the intellectuals of India, and Mahatma Gandhi led the "nonviolent" faction.

The place where the duo met has a stone with the history written on it. This location has now become a parking lot. Just beneath the stone is a place for sleeping. People who sleep there probably don't realize the importance of this spot and the story behind it. A Banyan tree sapling planted by Mahatma Gandhi in 1936 has endured the onslaught of time to give shade to many passers-by. An example of this is a large Banyan tree in the locality, and I was there many years ago. Today, I live on Banyan Court in my chosen town in Florida. Coincidence?

Mahatma Gandhi was born to parents of the Vaishnavas Sect of Hinduism, in the city of Porandar, Gujarat, on October 2, 1869. He was greatly influenced by the sect of Jainism. Gandhi was assassinated on January 30, 1948, in the compound of Birla House in New Delhi by a Hindu fanatic named Nathuram Godse, just four years before the Sanders family arrived in New Delhi in 1952.

His wife, Kasturba Makhanji Gandhi, lived from April 11, 1869, until Feb. 22, 1944.

Kathmandu, Nepal

Once things were organized for us to go to Nepal, we flew off to Patna, India. This waystation with an airport was our connecting point to Kathmandu. In Patna, we spent the night with an accommodating American family named Curry, of all things.

After this brief respite, we flew into the Kathmandu Airdrome in a four-engine Constellation plane. The dirt landing strip ended in a steep drop-off. In other words, a cliff! The pilot reversed thrust and managed not to go over the drop-off! How my breakfast stayed down, I will never know!

How did I feel about all these new experiences? I must say, after the abrupt experiences in New Delhi, followed by Lucknow, as I look back, I am not sure if I was brave enough to see the truth of the beggars, food that gave me diarrhea, etc. I was the eldest of four children, ten years and under, and I was not able to see their fear. There was such a curtailing of my own emotions as I knew this experience was to be for five years, or so. When one is ten, five additional years have no parameters.

Nepal, a landlocked country a little smaller than the State of Illinois, is bordered by Tibet and China to the north, India to the south, with Sikkim and West Bengal to the east. The country has a diverse geography, including fertile plains, subalpine forested hills, and eight of the world's ten tallest mountains, including Mount Everest, the highest point on Earth. Kathmandu is the capital and the largest city. The closest sea to Kathmandu is the Bay of Bengal on the Indian Ocean. Mount Everest is on the border Nepal shares with Tibet/China. The total population was less than ten million when the Sanders family arrived.

Parliamentary democracy was introduced in 1951.

Modern education in Nepal began with the opening of the first school in 1853. This school was only for the members of the ruling families and their courtiers. Schooling for the general population began only after 1951, when a popular movement ended the autocratic Rana family regime and started a democratic system.

There were about 300 schools and two colleges in 1951.

Nepal was strictly an agricultural country until 1950. In 1951 it entered the modern era. Agriculture was still the major economic activity, though only about 20% of the area was cultivable. Rice and wheat were the main food crops. Total population was less than ten million when the Sanders family arrived. With a total area of about 56,800 square miles, Nepal was founded by a feudal system in the 1700s. It is considered a Hindu country, although our cook was Buddhist, of which there are many in Nepal.

In 1952, there were only two ways to get into Kathmandu: by air or by foot. An Indian railway came as close to Nepal as it could considering the rough terrain. Neither a railroad nor a road for vehicles had yet been built to traverse the Himalayan Mountains into Nepal. So, from the end of the Indian railway line, barefoot coolies hand-carried my father's brand new 1952 Chevrolet as well as our household goods.

Two crews, about sixty men in total, carried the car and other supplies on footpaths over the Himalayas from the Indian end of the railroad, and last stop, into the Kathmandu Valley. They took off the car's wheels, put the chassis on bamboo poles, placed the poles on their shoulders, and carried it. Two teams of coolies changed off periodically, to relieve each other. The picture shows the windows rolled down. How nice to have Indian and Nepali dust collected and spread all over inside! We learned that this was not the first vehicle to have arrived in the Kathmandu Valley, carried in this way.

Prior to the recent arrival of the five families of the American Mission, the US government sent some Army-style four-wheel-drive Willys Jeeps. They, too, were carried in by barefoot coolies from the train tracks near the Indian/Nepali border.

When the American USOM offices at Ravi Bawhan received word that my dad's Chevrolet had arrived just over the border of Nepal and India, there was great excitement. Mrs. Wilcox (from Iowa) said that she would take a few of us children out to see the spectacle. I went right along with my Brownie Box camera.

Even more interesting, in 1940, because the King Tribhuvan had no motor transportation, Adolph Hitler sent the king a new 1939 Mercedes. That Mercedes had been carried in the very same way that my father's Chevrolet was brought in! The difference was that in 1940, the King had all the roads to himself. By 2020, though, there would be more than 500,000 vehicles in Nepal, including motorcycles, running in a road network of about 17,000 km. (10,625 miles). Tribhuvan Highway runs for 98 miles.

To house the new Foreign Service families, the US Government rented a palace compound from the Rana family, Nepal's former royalty that had been deposed in a coup. Within the walled compound were two large palaces: Rabi Bhawan and Kali Mati. A wall with a keyhole pass-through stood between the grounds of the two palaces.

Life Is a Stamp Collection

The Sanders family was temporarily assigned a location in Rabi Bhawan Palace. Actually, it was just one long, large room. There was no bathroom. Behind a screen in one corner was a pot, which we called a "honey bucket." It served as the toilet for our whole family—my parents and their four children—until a few weeks later, when we moved over to Kali Mati Palace.

Families jockeyed for housing options within the compound in Kali Mati (Black Earth). My mother especially liked the "Queen's apartment," which had a nice, rounded balcony, a fireplace, and a view of a Hindu yard temple. The Wilcox family, with three children, measured the space in each of the two available apartments. The Queen's apartment had slightly less space than the other. Mrs. Wilcox really wanted the larger apartment in Kali Mati. My mother's wish came true.

The rooms in our spacious apartment in Kali Mati had lovely marble floors. However, there was neither hot water nor central heat. And in Kathmandu, nestled in a valley in the Himalayan Mountains, it was ever so cold. Each room had kerosene heaters which emitted pungent fumes. Sometimes the wick would climb inside the kerosene heater and smoke up the beautiful carved ceiling. Then, a man of the "sweeper caste" would lob rags toward the ceiling and clean it promptly. All this while being watched by the wives on the oil paintings of the Rana male who had previously lived there with them. The chance to live in a royal palace may sound exciting, but Kali Mati Palace was not at all comfortable. On the positive side, it housed mostly families with children.

An empty marble-floored ballroom was located on a lower level, and during the monsoon, I would ride my American bicycle around and around the empty ballroom. The doors were open to the outside and the pounding of the rain might have seemed monotonous to some, but I found the sound of the water dulled one's sense of reality.

Rabi Bhawan Palace housed the Mission's offices; the family of Paul Rose, the "head man," some couples with older, teenage children, and single female secretaries. There were also rooms for visitors from New Delhi or the States.

Over in Kali Mati, Mother set about making a home for us in the Queen's apartment. She used the Danish Modern furniture that the US State Department issued, along with some interesting newly found items from local bazaars. Months later, when our overland shipments of crates of personal things arrived, we had a spinet piano, World Books, Nancy Drew novels for me, and clothes to grow into.

Once our home was established in Kathmandu, invitations started coming in for all the adult Americans from King Tribhuvan's Ministers and the Court. The British Embassy extended invitations for what amounted to a new social type of life that most Americans had never known in their home country. I was usually included, since the Ambassador from Great Britain had a daughter, Margo, who was close to my age. Margo had a horse which she let me ride. What a thrill it was, riding this horse as it cantered around the Embassy's riding ring.

At the frequent informal teas at the British Embassy at 4 p.m., I often listened quietly as the ballet dancer, Boris Lissanevitch, recounted his tales about his escape out of Russia and his first marriage to Kira, who was a dancer as well. The two of them were with the Ballet Russe. Ballet dancer, master chef, hotelier, tiger hunter, fighter pilot and trapeze artist, the list that describes Boris Lissanevitch is endless. He was a man you would meet once and never forget.

At ten years old in 1952, I sat behind Boris's wicker chair on the grassy lawn and always wanted to hear more! I was spellbound. Perhaps his stories are what fueled my wanderlust.

In 1942, Boris was up in Simla (now Shimla) hunting when he got the news about the Sepoy Mutiny war. He hastily set about returning to Calcutta, by rail, accompanying the sick wife of a friend. All along the way, they encountered burned out rail stations. There was no food or water, and they could not get off at the stations or they would be murdered or kidnapped. The riots in India were the result of the Indians who had endured British Rule for two centuries.

When he arrived, Boris found a changed Calcutta as military activity preparations were all about. American soldiers flocked to Calcutta, which became a major center of the US Tenth Air Force.

Suddenly, the jungles of Assam and Simla, where Boris had hunted, were now of high importance. The Burma Road was under heavy attack and was soon cut off, isolating China, Saigon, Rangoon, and several other ports. It looked as if Calcutta would be next on the Japanese route.

The only way to free China was by air, and thus began history's most famous air lift. Courageous pilots took off from runways hastily laid in Assam and flew over "the Hump" of the Tibetan and Chinese Himalayas.

In Calcutta, during the beginning of the 2nd World War, many Americans gathered there in Boris's "300 Club," which became a major center of the US Tenth Air Force. He and Kira had an apartment above the club. They had a child, a girl, and Boris's mother, Maria Alexandrovna Lissanevitch, came from France to join her son. Boris recounted that after many adventures and experiences putting on shows of dancing around the area of India and Indonesia, his marriage to Kira ended.

(Later in Nepal, Boris married a young girl, Inga, who

was Danish and twenty-three years his junior. Boris and Inga had two sons.)

"Overnight the 300 Club was invaded," Boris wrote, "by generals and colonels." At the end of the Club gardens, a hanger-like structure was built, and it was called "Monsoon Square Gardens." Entertainers from England and America came and gave a welcome comedic relief from the daily bombings for the soldiers.

Brigadier General Frank Haggett was a frequent guest. He also became a big game enthusiast, and Boris took him to Cooch Behar, where the General was quite lucky to bag two tigers.

On the arrival of the 10th Air Force in Bengal, the Maharaja of Cooch Behar turned over his private airport to them as a training ground for the young Americans.

This was all going on just as I was born in Feb. 1942. I would not meet Boris for another ten years and in the Nepali Himalayas.

Fast forward to Kathmandu ten years later, with me, at the British Embassy, sitting on the lawn. As tea was served by the servants, grownups of several nationalities sat and talked and recounted their adventures and misadventures.

Many years later while visiting my parents in Martin, Tennessee, just by chance, I saw in a local newspaper that "Boris Lissanevitch of Kathmandu," as he was known, had died. He had opened a hotel, "The Royal" and, within it, a bar called the "Yak and Yeti." He was famous, not just for his patience in trying to help to mountaineers but also in trying to obtain permits for their mountain adventures. He also put a pig farm together for himself.

The King counted on Boris to obtain liquor and other commodities from Calcutta for himself and various dignitaries. If an inbound plane was late in arriving at the Kathmandu airdrome with the King's dinner necessities, there was much consternation that earned Boris some eye rolling.

Even more years later, a fellow flight attendant, Connie

Friedman told me that she had been to Kathmandu and stayed at Boris's hotel. On the day of departure, she and her husband stopped in at the "Yak and Yeti" for a departure drink. Connie soon found out that the ice cubes had not been made from bottled water! It was quite the miserable trip home.

In 1952 in Kathmandu, one of our pastimes was listening as a group to the wireless for presidential election news and other noteworthy events back in the States. Lowell Thomas was a prominent newscaster. That name would stay with me. I now have a few autographed first editions of his work. They provide a virtual connection with my rather strange childhood passages.

There was not a lot for children to do, so I became an avid kite flyer. We children would buy beautiful rice paper kites with Nepali designs. I soon learned how to grind up glass, mix flour and water with the glass, and rub it up and down the kite string.

I would navigate my kite aloft from the high balcony of our home in Kali Mati Palace. The weaving and waving of the kite in the evening sun would attract an opponent. Quickly, a similar kite would be in the sky, coming close to my kite. The competition was on! Now, we just had to get the glass-encrusted strings to come together to begin the sawing created by the momentum of the wind. Which one of us would be the winner? Quite often I was. Other times my kite would be cut off, and into the late evening sky it would go, ever so high, caught up with the wind. Upward and onward. Was that a metaphor for my life to come as a flight attendant?

Current Day Nepal

In 1954 my family was invited to participate in the ceremony celebrating the opening of Tribhuvan Road. I was the only one from our family able to go to the ceremony. I sat beside one of the teenage Nepali princesses. She spoke English and was very nice to me. We chatted as we waited for hours for the event to begin.

Things have changed a lot since then. The country now has many young girls being taken out under the guise of being educated, but, they will be sold into sex slavery. Each year, along this road, approximately 7,000 -15,000 girls around the age of seven are captured or misled about their destination. Many end up in the Middle East. Many girl children are still considered not worthy of schooling by many uneducated families.

Demi Moore travelled to Nepal and was photographed at the exit point from Nepal into India. As many celebrities do, she took up this issue and tried to bring awareness of this sex trafficking.

The Middle Eastern men are known for taking sex trips to Bangkok for several days. There is just too much horror to comprehend about the lack of other people's Divine rights.

꩜

One time, when my mother was visiting me in Los Angeles, California from Martin, Tennessee, she read in an LA paper the story of a love affair that developed between a Saudi man and an American woman, named Marianne Alireza. They had met at the University of California at Berkley. Mother said that I would probably enjoy reading the newspaper article.

I did. It detailed on how Marianne escaped with her children from Saudi into Switzerland.

A few weeks later, on a working flight, a fellow flight attendant, Kay Smith, from Salt Lake City, came up from her jump seat and said, "Angela, there is a woman sitting across from my jump seat at 3R, and I think you would enjoy talking with her as she illegally took her children out of Saudi Arabia into Switzerland."

Wow! I knew the story! It was the same lady from Berkeley who had been written about in the newspaper.

I was able to have quite a nice conversation with her. She had a cast on her leg. She said that her children had given her a bicycle, and she'd had an accident. By then her children were back in Saudi Arabia, and she stated that they had a working relationship.

Life Is a Stamp Collection

Marianne wrote a book, *At the Drop of a Veil*, due to the encouragement of a man who was seated next to her at a dinner party, John Kenneth Galbraith!

I knew the name John Kenneth Galbraith. He had been Ambassador to India in 1961-1963. I had graduated from Stewardess College in Ft. Worth, Texas in 1963, about six years after we left as a family from Simla, India.

Galbraith served under President Kennedy from 1961 to 1963. His rapport with JFK was such that he regularly bypassed the State Department and sent diplomatic cables directly to the President. John Kenneth was a Canadian American economist, public official, and intellectual. I remember somewhere he wrote "Swatting flies, raising hell, this is India!"

I told Maryanne a bit of my story and asked if she would let me pay for two copies of her book and autograph them and mail them to me.

She did! The book was so very interesting, but it was very unlike my story as she was an adult when her life took a very divergent and different course!

Chapter Two

How we ended up in Nepal

Point Four in President Harry S. Truman's inaugural address on January 20, 1949 was, "We must embark on a bold new program for making the benefits of our scientific advances and industrial progress available for the improvement and growth of underdeveloped areas." President Truman appointed Chester Bowles as Ambassador to both India and Nepal.

The US Congress passed the Point Four Program in May 1950. The primary mission was to improve the living conditions of the receiving country through technical assistance in health, education, and agriculture. What the Marshall Plan had done for the war-torn countries of Europe and Asia, the Point Four Program would attempt to do for less-developed countries worldwide.

My father, Everette N. Sanders, was part of the first wave of Foreign Service technical assistance officers to go to the Hindu/Buddhist nation under the Point Four Program. We were one of the first five initial US families to be assigned to Kathmandu.

Daddy's work would focus on helping Nepalese farmers become more efficient in producing food for their people. The mission was to help relieve hunger and poverty in this nation of mostly impoverished people.

In addition to his desire to help the people in poorer

countries, the salary and amenities were a major reason for his joining the Foreign Service. His game plan was to save enough money while overseas to provide his children with college educations. He eventually sent all four children to college, a first for the extended Sanders family.

My parents were both of very fine European stock—German and Scottish—with an apparent latent bent for adventure.

Daddy was born in 1913, the son of a farming family in Arkansas. He was the only one of eight who went to college. He graduated as a rural sociologist from the University of Arkansas after transferring from Arkansas A&M.

He became a county agent in Mena, a small hamlet nestled in the Ouachita Mountains in Arkansas. There, he met a lovely brunette who had been voted the "Prettiest Girl in Mena High School." My mother, Winifred Craig, was working as a telephone operator. She grew up her entire younger life in the small town of Mena. It was a typical small settlement of hard-working, amiable, originally European people, just trying to meld with a post-pioneer adventuring/settling society. My grandparents joined the First Baptist church, built a home outside the city limits, put in a fishpond, and had chickens. My mother told me about gathering eggs as a child, reaching up into the nest and feeling something warm, which turned out to be a snake that had swallowed an egg. There was a long clothesline for hanging out the Monday wash. That line was still there when I spent summers with my grandparents.

My father was so different from the local boys. Everette and Winifred fell in love and married in a Baptist church ceremony on February 22, 1941. They settled in and started raising a family. A year later, on February 17, I was born in Searcy, Arkansas.

Life was good. Later they shifted to Mount Ida, near Hot Springs, Arkansas, where my brother, Craig, was born in the Army-Navy Hospital in Hot Springs. At three years of age, I decided that this little brother was here to stay, as they never returned him to the hospital.

One day a friend of my mother's called her to say, "Angela

is standing by the highway where the road to my house joins up with the Hot Springs highway." I had my dad's old leather suitcase which had been given to him when he left Texarkana for college. Apparently at age three, for some reason or other, I had had enough. That same year, my mother told me to watch Craig on the front porch. When she came back, he had rolled off the edge of the porch. I explained that I had told him not to move.

Shortly thereafter, Daddy accepted an assignment in Paragould, Arkansas, where Brenda and Roger, my youngest siblings, were born. All my father's assignments during World War II had to do with improving agricultural practices. He extended advice to local Arkansas farmers.

I remember grocery rationing and going to the corner store for my mother and buying margarine with a big red dot, which I later would mash it up to color the margarine.

In those days, entertainment was driving to the Missouri border on a hot Sunday afternoon to buy Popsicles and gas for the car at a nickel less per gallon after crossing over the Missouri River. On these trips, we drove through wealthy farmers' fields.

African Americans worked the fields in the hot sun. Their little black children would stand beside the road and wave as we drove by in Daddy's black, sloped-back Chevrolet. Once, I called "Chocolate drop!" out the window. My mother told me that was not very nice. I had no concept of political correctness.

Across the fields of waving grasses, cotton fields, and soybean crops, we could see shanty-type shacks where these laborers lived. There was a TV antenna on the roof and a Cadillac parked outside the shanty. We didn't have either, but I can understand why they did.

This was the setting in those days that made the complete picture for people who were not yet considered equal.

Traveling at least forty-five miles per hour in the car, the hot summer breeze would lift some of the stifling heat off the backs of our necks, and from the hanging our heads out the windows, the wind tangled our hair. We loved every breath of it!

One day my father came home for lunch and showed

Mother a brochure that had come from Washington, DC. The government was seeking agricultural people to go to India to help with better farming practices, as people there were starving, not only there, but in many other places in the world. After much talk and consternation about taking their young family to a land about which they knew little, they decided to become members of the US Foreign Service. My Mother's answer, "Why not?" To Asia it was. Thus began our world adventures.

However, we would end up in the Nepalese Himalayas instead of India. Here I would meet British adventurers, Americans from Iowa, US doctors who were opening much-needed clinics, more Americans, museum bird specimen hunters, minor royalty, and many Delhi visitors.

I remember many horrible shots—inoculations against cholera, typhoid, typhus, and more. We children would place cold washcloths over the swollen areas from the injections, potato-sized bumps on our arms.

I overheard my parents talking about putting my dog, Pepper, to sleep, so I wrote my grandfather and asked him if he would take Pepper. He did.

There were going-away parties, including one at our First Baptist Church. Most folks probably thought we were going to Africa rather than India. I did. After all, the churches were always talking about missionaries in Africa. I hoped to see "natives" like in the comic books. I was so disappointed when I found out that *natives* referred to Africa, not India. I just didn't quite know how to think about that country. In school, we hadn't studied about India yet. I knew about New York and its skyscrapers but not a place so far away as India.

We travelled in our new car, towards Washington, DC, seeing historical sights all along the way, which fueled an appreciation of the American past of our unique history.

Now in Washington, DC, and living in an apartment in Lafayette Circle sometimes as I was studying in the front window of our two-story apartment, I watched limousines go by with beautiful, lovely-gowned ladies as passengers. I wondered if, by chance, they were Margert and Bess Truman. Daydreaming was a part of balancing this new life as a ten-year-old.

As our home was a Southern Baptist home, there were no playing cards. Yes, even when travelling and taking up residence in the odd Himalaya. However, I suppose that my parents realized the need to keep us occupied in Asia, so they went to a local drug store and purchased jigsaw puzzles and playing cards to take to India with us.

Finally, after my father's orientation was finished in Washington, DC, we flew to India.

What it was like in Nepal

The Nepal valley of Kathmandu was visually a contradiction. I was too young to appreciate beauty in even the most bizarre opposites of my young experiences. The buildings were mostly brown with carvings and balconies.

I, the eldest, helped Mother look after my three siblings. Craig, next to me, was seven. Brenda was five, and Roger was three. On special occasions, like birthday parties, my brothers and sister and I, played with King Tribhuvan's grandchildren.

Paul Rose was head of the Foreign Service team in Nepal. I remember his wife, Mary, along with Bethel Fleming and other American wives, including my mother, for their pioneering spirit.

The Rose family sent their children to Woodstock, an American missionary school in India. But Woodstock didn't have room for the Sanders children. So, Mother home-schooled us, using the Calvert system, out of Calvert, Maryland.

There was no American commissary in Nepal, as there was in Delhi, so we lived off the local economy. The only meats available in Kathmandu were tough cuts of water buffalo or mutton. Mother had our Nepalese cook pound the water buffalo meat with a machete. Then, Mother would dip it in eggs and flour, southern style, and cook it for a long time to make it reasonably edible. Cows were holy, and so were not a source of protein for us.

Our Buddhist cook kept his head shaved, as was

traditional, but he maintained a pigtail so that he could be pulled up to heaven in the event of his untimely death. My mother probably would have been a suspect if he suddenly disappeared.

Chapter Three

Climbing Mount Everest

A highlight of my time in Nepal was my meeting in April 1953 with Edmund Hillary and Tenzing Norkai, who, on May 29, 1953, were the first persons known to have climbed to the top of Nepal's Mount Everest. At 29,029 feet elevation, it was the tallest mountain in the world. They were part of the ninth British expedition to Everest, led by Sir John Hunt of England. A few other Americans and I went to see them off. I still have a picture of myself standing beside Sir John Hunt, the expedition leader, while Edmund Hillary was signing my autograph book. What a treasure! I also got Tenzing Norkai's autograph. I was eleven at the time and getting autographs, especially those of famous people, was the thing young girls did. I remember all the British climbers wearing wide-legged khaki walking shorts. As Hillary put his leg up to write in my little book against his knee, I could see the edge of his striped undershorts. I later told my dad that I had seen his undershorts peeping out from his khaki shorts. I thought nothing of it, except as an eleven-year-old, it was a big deal!

Later, when the climbing team returned to Kathmandu, the Americans extended an invitation to the entire group to come to Rabi Bhawan for a congratulatory reception. It was in one of the grand ballrooms in Rabi Bhawan.

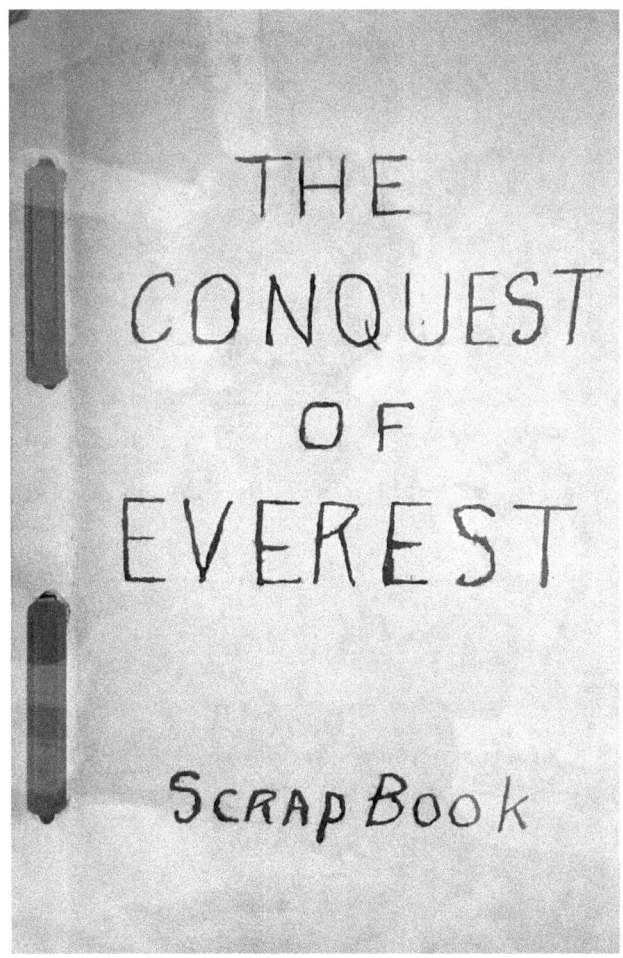

Dad brought Edmund Hillary over to me and asked me, right there in front of God and everybody, if this was the man whose striped undershorts I had seen. Apparently, my father did not realize that they were indeed undershorts! I was mortified, and to this day, still am, a bit. Again, I was just eleven.

Sir Edmund Hillary was absolutely my hero. I awarded him that title when he signed my autograph book at the jumping off place to climb Everest on a chilly Himalayan morning.

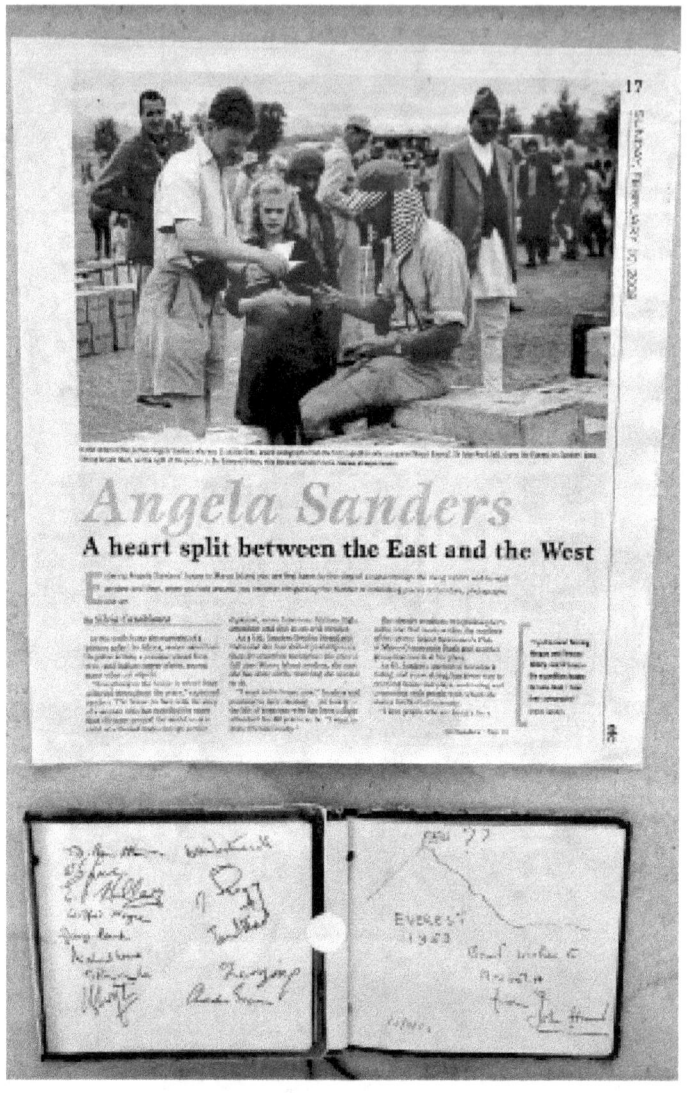

Edmund Hillary was born in 1919 in Auckland, New Zealand. Although he rose to great heights from climbing Mount Everest, he had described himself as "a small and a rather lonely child." Actually, he did grow to great heights, well over six feet and he took up beekeeping, and many years later he became a mountain climber. Sir Edmund Hillary was cited as "New Zealand's most trusted individual."

In 1952, Princess Elizabeth of England and her husband, Philip Mountbatten, were in Kenya when news of the death of

King George VI came. King Albert Frederick Arthur George, father to Princess Elizabeth and sister Princess Margaret of England, lived from December 14, 1895 to February 6, 1952. Elizabeth's coronation was held a year and a half later, to allow an appropriate length of time between a monarch's passing and holding a celebration to crown her as the heir. The conquest of Everest was announced on the eve of Elizabeth II's coronation on June 1, 1953.

This is the same year Hillary also married his wife, Louise Mary Rose. He subsequently wrote that he was embarrassed by the honor of being knighted by Queen Elizabeth as "it was truly a team effort." He did accept the knighthood, of course.

Having achieved international fame as the first known person to climb and summit Mount Everest, Hillary took up exploration. He reached the South Pole by tractor on January 4, 1958, as leader of the New Zealand division of the Commonwealth Trans-Antarctic Expedition.

He was among the first to scale Mount Herschel in the Antarctic expedition in 1967. In 1985, Sir Hillary and astronaut Neil Armstrong flew a small twin-engine plane to the North Pole, making Hillary the first person to stand at both poles and the summit of Everest, also known as the "third pole."

During the last fifty years of his life, Sir Edmund Hillary devoted himself to environmental and humanitarian efforts that made a profound difference to communities in Nepal, where his famous summiting was achieved. Sir Edmund continued to set up schools in outer areas of Nepal.

I recently saw a TV Special, and in a village of the higher Himalayas, there was a statue of the New Zealander with many Buddhist prayer scarves around his neck. It stands in the village of the higher Himalayas.

Hillary Family with my Dad (far right)

Sir Edmund Hillary's Devastating Loss

In 1975, Sir Edmund Hillary's wife's parents, Phyl and Jim, from New Zealand, were visiting the Hillary family in Kathmandu. During that time, Sir Edmund's wife Louise and daughter Belinda boarded a helicopter in Kathmandu to fly to a site north of the city to be with Edmund where he was on a job. The helicopter crashed on take-off in the Kathmandu Valley; both Louise and Belinda were killed.

The helicopter pilot had failed to remove pins that held the rotary blades in place. Because of strong Himalayan wind gusts, the pins were used to stabilize the craft while it was on the ground.

Later, in his book, *View from the Summit*, Sir Hillary wrote that the British Ambassador, Michael Scott, and his wife "were a tower of strength." They drove out to meet Edmund as he had been up country visiting at one of the schools that he had donated to Nepal. On the evening of the tragedy, Ambassador and Mrs. Scott drove him to a lovely spot beside the Bagmati River, the Holy River of Kathmandu Valley, where there were two funeral pyres. On top of each pyre was a body wrapped in white cloth. At a nod from the Ambassador, the wood and kindling were lighted. Sir Edmond wrote, "For half an hour, I watched my loved ones go up in flames."

On the way to the bazaars to buy supplies, my mother often drove us across the very same Bagmati River in our Willy's Jeep.

The Fabulous Flemings

One fond memory I have of the Fleming family is of Dr. Bethel Fleming and her daughter walking over the mountain pass from India into Nepal. Dr. Bob and his son, Bob, went off hunting birds for the Chicago Museum.

So, it was left to Dr. Bethel to arrange for their household goods and luggage to be transported by *lori* to the mountain pass as far as the road went. Dr. Bethel asked the *lori* driver if she and Sally Beth could ride in the truck as well. The driver refused them. He said he only contracted for luggage and furniture, not passengers. So, Dr. Bethel and Sally Beth had to walk over the mountains.

The coolies carried the goods down the same path over which the King's Mercedes and my dad's Chevrolet were transported. Somehow, the coolies got word to Rabi Bhawan that the Fleming women were coming in over Chandragiri Pass.

My mother and Donald Wilcox from Iowa, age twelve, drove out and met Sally Beth and Dr. Bethel in an American Jeep. Mother drove them in the Jeep from Thankot to Kathmandu, to Rabi Bhawan, to the luxury of American soap and a hot tub of water.

The "Fabulous Flemings" had arrived in Kathmandu in October 1953. Dr. Bethel Fleming was assigned to the United Medical Mission to Nepal. As a pre-teen, I volunteered to serve in her hospital. My job was to cut bed sheets and roll up narrow strips to be used for bandages. That will give you an idea of the rudimentary nature of health care in Nepal.

My siblings and I played with the Flemings' daughter, Sally Beth, who was more my younger sister's age than mine. Sally's brother, Bob, was away in Woodstock School.

The Fleming family, with Angela at top right

I felt lucky to have been with Dr. Bob Sr. on an expedition to collect rare species of Himalayan birds for the museum. He knew more about the birds of the Himalayas than any other person. He collected 700 species for the Chicago Natural History Museum.

Once Dr. Bob let several of us accompany him in Jeeps on a journey up into the mountainsides. The Jeeps went as far as the road lasted, then we walked farther as Dr. Bob looked for rare and special species of Himalayan birds. I was absolutely awed to have been with him as he collected these rare birds.

Mrs. Walker, a wife of another USOM advisor, decided to go along. She hired a *dandi,* an elevated seat like a palanquin with poles resting on the shoulders of four men, to carry her most of the way. In those days, a thirty-five-year-old was really quite old to a young girl. Mrs. Walker let me ride part of the way in the *dandi*, while she took a turn at climbing. Walking *up* hill all the time gets boring and tiring! Anyway, in the evenings on this trek, we sat around an open fire while servants set up tents and prepared our meals. In the beautiful mountain air, I listened with interest to the adults describing their Asian experiences. If I turned my head just right, I could avoid, or at least minimize, the smell of the dried cow-dung patties that were burning as energy to cook the dinner. In addition to being used as cooking fuel, the patties while still damp were mixed with mud to form a cement to insulate the outside of villagers' homes. As part of their chores, Nepali children followed the water buffalo and the many wandering holy cows, picking up the patties then taking them home to be used for fuel or cement.

While my mother was visiting her sister in Temple, Texas in 1990, they went to a bookstore where Mother bought Grace Nies Fletcher's book, *The Fabulous Flemings of Kathmandu*. Mother wrote inside the book, which I now have, "Bought from Church Library sale, February 20, 1990." The book expresses beautifully the rich, full lives of those two Christian missionaries and other families.

In 2020, I received word that Dr. Bethel had a bad fall at her daughter, Sally Beth's home. This apparently was sometime back around 1976. After the fall and some recovery, Bethel and Sally Beth visited the Maharani of Tehri. It is written "returning through the bazaar, in a four-passenger rickshaw, it broke. The women were dropped, their legs flailed in the air." Dr. Bethel later died from sustained injuries from that fall.

It goes on to mention Bruce Fiol, who accompanied Dr. Bob on another bird hunting expedition. They had to throw a lighted ember into the cave where they intended to bed down for the night as a bear had beaten them to the cave. It worked, the bear left. So the lesson is: if a bear has already arrived in your cave, throw in an ember!

In 1988, when I arrived onto Marco Island, Bruce Fiol was the minister at our local Presbyterian Church. He and I had attended Woodstock School in Mussoorie, India but in different years!

Church Fellowship

In Kathmandu, my dad and the heads of the other four families decided that they should have some kind of Sunday worship service in Rabi Bhawan Palace. The service was definitely "looser" than Arkansas Southern Baptists would have liked. However, it seemed not to offend anyone, and it gave this little Foreign Service group a cementing of fellowship for their intended purpose of helping the people of this nation of Nepal.

This is where I learned that there was someone other than a Baptist, *ever so moral*; a Methodist, the consensus was that they had 'slid a bit,' because they could dance; and Catholic. You don't even want to know the stories which centered around the fact that they could both dance and drink!

In our Sunday afternoon drives to see different Hindu and Buddhist temples, I was exposed a bit to those different religions. I began to understand tolerance by the Hindus and Buddhists for us as Christians. I am sure we all agree that this kind of tolerance should be for all mankind, beginning with Christianity. However, sadly, the rigidity of Middle Eastern religions, including Christianity, has seemingly a long way to go.

After living in Nepal, I learned that Buddha is not to be worshiped. His teachings can accompany any religion. Buddha said, "Don't do these things because I teach them, but use these teachings to enhance your spirit and actions toward yourself and others." "Do not judge, but observe, digest and allow others to do the same. Don't impose your will on others but let them find their own spiritual awakening." I have wondered if our Ten Commandments came from Buddhism, as they do not believe in violence and that religion is about 500 years older than Christianity.

When I was eleven or twelve, our family took a trip to Pakistan and Afghanistan. Daddy, in one of his "Oh, let's give the kids some experiences that will broaden them so much" attitudes, decided that we needed to see Khyber Pass.

In a filthy Pakistani train station, we had a seven-hour—*I swear, seven hours*—layover connection in the middle of the night. There was no place for kids to lie down, or even to sit without smelling a urinal. The only thing worse was finally getting on a sooty train.

On the way from Pakistan to Afghanistan, I was fascinated as we went through historic Khyber Pass. It was well worth the harshness of travel to get there. There were rock/brick walls with square openings for rifles along the way. It is the most northerly and important pass between and bordering Pakistan and Afghanistan. Due to the width, this Khyber Pass, being in the Himalayas, has long been a physical and cultural divide between South and Central Asia. It has seen many invasions of troops by large numbers of armies going to invade the subcontinent. Comparatively broad mountain passes are located south of the Kabul River. Kabul is pronounced *COB-ble*, unlike State Department newbies who call it *Ka-BULL*.

I had been told a story of how an American woman wanted to put her foot through a shambly border fence and just touch her toe to the Afghan side. On the other side of the fence, Afghan soldiers wearing Russian uniforms quickly pointed their Russian rifles toward her and her marauding foot.

I thought it would be really swell if I could do that. Well, you would have thought war had broken out as Daddy really fussed at me in no uncertain terms when I tried to put my leg through to the other side of the fence. Parents can be so restricting sometimes with the *one* child they have who wants to go with the wind rather than be normal and anchored.

We somehow made it back home, via India, and hopped on a flight into the Kathmandu Airdrome, landing again on the one runway which stopped at the tippy top of a mountain edge.

In 1954, when I was twelve, we visited Srinagar, the summer capital of Kashmir. Jammu is the winter capital. Each holds the title for six months at a time.

Kashmir's meaning is *desiccated land* from the Sanskrit *Ka* meaning water and *shimeera* meaning to desiccate.

We arrived in June, and Dad rented a houseboat for us to live on for about a week. It seems that we hired a cook to come and deliver our meals, arriving by boat at the appointed times!

One day my parents hired a boat to take us around the lake, and we saw floating chunks of land with unique and common plants, on them. Little islands of their own.

The colorful house boats were quite a delight for my eyes. At one point, I drifted off to sleep floating in the sunshine. As I reflect, I must have finally felt that I could relax, and not have to be so on guard and protect my younger siblings, as the sounds of Delhi and Kathmandu were now far back in memories past. This would be the last time I could let my guard down and totally relax. When one is the eldest of four children, and I saw how frightened my parents were, over-protecting us, and not letting us out into the bazaars like the other American parents, I knew my life would be forever a preparation for more challenges.

Of course, when I was chosen to be a stewardess for American Airlines just eleven short years later, I didn't realize that there would be a life of constant diligence as well. As I reflect back on all this, my life certainly did arrive in a wave protection of blessings!

History of Himalayas and Kashmir

In the past century, the east coast of the United States has moved about eight feet further away from Europe. Here is a little background information on the Himalayas.

Fossils of sea and coastal creatures can still be found in the Himalayas, as it was once two coast lines that merged.

These fossils not only provide evidence that the Himalayas once existed on a coastline, but also information about climate change and tectonic plate movement.

The name for the Himalayas comes from the Sanskrit *him* for snow and *alaya* for dwelling, essentially, the home of the snow. Mount Everest is named after George Everest, one of the surveyor generals of India. It was not, however, Everest, who first surveyed the mountain, but Andrew Waugh who took over the role of surveyor general after Everest. Waugh thought it would be a good idea to name the mountain after his predecessor. Everest did not like the idea, but he was overruled, and his name was eventually adopted for the mountain by the Royal Geographical Society in 1865.

Since 1921, prior to Hillary and Norgay's notorious and successful climb in 1953, several dozen attempts had been undertaken to climb to the peak. Since 1953, nearly 3,000 people have accomplished the feat and around 200 have died trying.

The Himalayas serve as a climatic divide as well as a physical barrier between India and the rest of the continent. They prevent cold winter winds from entering India in the winter, making India warmer than other regions along the same lines of latitude at that same time of the year. Similarly, they prevent the southern monsoon winds from taking moisture across the border into Tibet; the result is India gets far more precipitation than the relatively arid Tibet. The Himalayas are notable not only for their size but for their structure. The Himalayas are considered fold-mountains as they consist of a series of jagged peaks that are mostly parallel, as though they have been folded over and over again. They are also home to deep ravines, glaciers, and rivers, forming a complex and treacherous range. Kashmir sits at an elevation of 5,200 feet, in its own region of the Indian subcontinent.

The Himalayas are home to some interesting creatures: clouded leopards, Asiatic black bears, tahrs, and langurs to name a few. Snow leopards and brown bears have adapted to live at higher elevations. Unfortunately, due to human interest and interference, many species that call the Himalayas home are dying out, such as the Indian rhinoceros and the Kashmir stag.

While you might not think the icy mountain peaks of the Himalayas that you see in photos would be conducive to growing much of anything, the little hidden valleys of the Himalayan range are actually vital for food production. Farmers grow apples, cherries, grapes, oranges, pears, almonds, walnuts, tea, and a variety of herbs and spices in and around the range.

The earliest recorded history of Kashmir begins at the time of the Mahabharata Epoch. In the third century BC, Emperor Asoka introduced Buddhism in the valley. This epoch was from 3067 BCE to Modi era, as of today in 2022 AD.

Kashmir became a major hub of Hindu culture by the ninth century AD. It was the birthplace of the Hindu sect called Kashmiri Shaivism and a haven for the greatest Sanskrit scholars!

I read that after centuries of Hindu and Buddhist rule, Muslim Moghul emperors took control of Kashmir in the fifteenth century, converted the population to Islam and incorporated it into the Islamic Moghul empire. Islamic Moghul rule should not be confused with modern forms of authoritarian Islamic regimes.

The contemporary, more authoritarian, form of Moghul rule dates from 1846 when by the treaties of Lahore and Amritsar at the conclusion of the First Sikh War, Raja Gulab Singh, the Dogra ruler of Jammu was created. This was for the Maharaja (ruling prince) of an extensive but somewhat ill-defined Himalayan kingdom to the east of the River Indus and west of the River Ravi.

Dogra refers to the Hindu people of Indo-Arian ethno-linguistic group in India and Pakistan who are one of a group of hill dwellers in the Dogra district between Punjab and Kashmir.

A few facts regarding the River Indus: The Indus River is one of the very important rivers in the world, running across three major Asian nations, Tibet, India, and Pakistan. It originates near the Mansarovar Lake in the Tibetan plateau. It moves through Tibet and India and runs most of its course through Pakistan, making it the longest river in Pakistan. I remember studying about the various rivers of India when I was in Auckland House School in Simla. The origin of the Indus in the Himalayas always seemed rather spiritual to the people.

The Indus, like many rivers around the world, faces numerous challenges. The most important is the pollution which goes into the world's rivers. Also, there is the concern about the falling water levels due to rise in the world's temperatures.

When we lived in Kathmandu, we crossed the Baghmati River to go into the bazaars in the interior of Kathmandu. Bodies were cremated, and then the ashes were shoved into the river. All around were people bathing in the holy river, brushing their teeth, spitting the water into the river, then washing their hair, heedless of the pollution within those waters.

When there was an epidemic and people were dying too quickly, a cinder was placed into the mouth of the dead body, and they were shoved into the river to float downstream.

The Nepalese Government

King Tribhuvan Bir Bikram Shah Dev, better known as King Tribhuvan, ascended the throne at the age of five upon his father's death on December 11, 1911. He was a progressive monarch with two Queens, Kanti and Ishwari, who were sisters. He ruled Nepal from the time we arrived until he died at age forty-eight on March 13, 1955, the same year the Sanders family left Nepal. His mother, Her Majesty Queen Dibyaswori Rajya Laxmi Devi Shah, who had brought up Tribhuvan in a very congenial environment, acted as regent for the first few years of Tribhuvan's reign. However, the position of monarch was mainly titular; the real power was with the Rana family, which supplied Nepal with its hereditary prime minister, until the family was deposed in a coup.

My parents were often invited to the Royal Palace, called Singha Durbar, for functions. My mother had a beautiful yellow chiffon ball gown, which made her look so stunning with her dark hair!

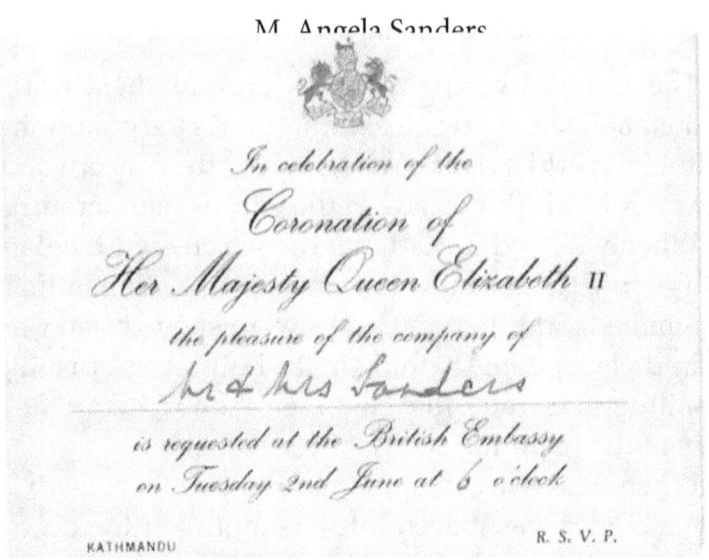

King Tribhuvan was quite receptive to being entertained inside the American apartments. I have a photo of him and some of his gentlemen entourage, standing in the Queen's Drawing Room in Kali Mati, which was our living room. On these occasions, guests were met by Mohan, our bearer, who wore an ornate headdress and a very regal white serving jacket. As I peeped through a keyhole at all the "important" adults, I could tell that Mohan was so proud, holding his highly shined copper tray with a crisp monogrammed ecru napkin.

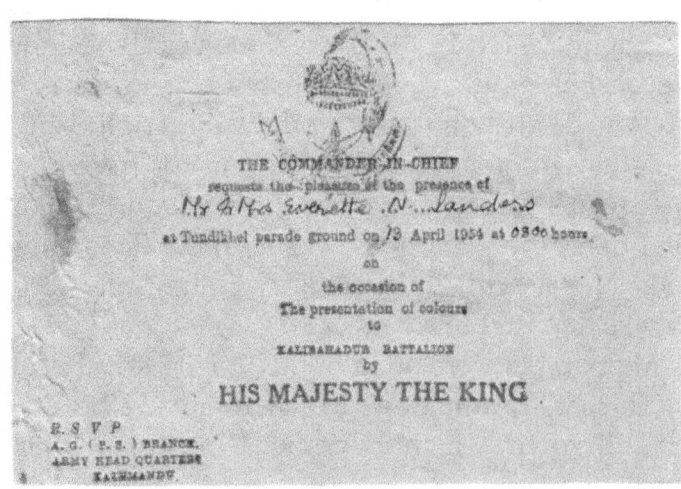

My Southern Baptist parents did not serve or keep liquor in our home. So, when the King was in our home, Mohan served him V-8 juice in small, elegant cocktail glasses on his tray. The

King had his Scotch flown in regularly from Calcutta on Indian Airlines.

During the time that we were in Nepal, King Tribhuvan instituted a more democratic regime. But because the King was reluctant to assert a forceful role for the monarchy, the Government of India found it necessary to serve as the power behind the throne in the Nepalese government whenever tough decisions had to be made.

He was succeeded by his son, King Mahendra, whose coronation was in 1956. King Mahendra was a well-educated, ambitious person. He decided to remove the bureaucratic system and improve the political process of the country. He introduced a parliamentary constitution on his own initiative, which was modeled on India's democratic system.

Preparing to Leave Nepal

When it came time to prepare to leave Kathmandu, word went out via the servants' grapevine, all the way to the Royal Family. One of the King's younger sons contacted my mother and made arrangements to stop by our apartment to see our furniture, books, dolls, and other items that we were willing to sell. He purchased everything in one fell swoop. He apparently went home to the Royal Palace, Singa Durbar, and bragged to his eldest brother, Prince Mahendra.

A few days later, on a bright, sunshiny day, there was a knock at our outer gate and door. Our servant came to tell Mother that Crown Prince Mahendra's representative wanted to speak to her.

Mother quickly straightened from the packing of things we definitely would take home to the States. She received the representative who stated to her that the Crown Prince "desires all your household goods: piano, books, World Books, lesson books and lesson plans, all toys, *everything* that is for sale."

Mother politely explained that everything had already been sold to the Crown Prince's younger brother.

"Madam," the representative made a more emphatic statement, "The Crown Prince DESIRES all your goods!"

With that, Mother realized that royal ranking is royal ranking. The Crown Prince got the goods.

Except for the Chevrolet.

A banker had approached Daddy early on and asked that he not let it be known that the car was for sale, as the King would want it, and all things the King wanted, the King would get. The banker paid cash for the 1952 Chevrolet when we left in 1955.

In 2001, King Birendra Shah Dev, the grandson of the King Tribhuvan, son of Crown Prince Mahendra, who "desired our household goods," was eating with his family. Apparently, this son was angry about his mother not approving of his choice for marriage. So, Birendra's young prince, high on drugs, shot and killed all the ruling family. This led to a change of the custom of having a ruling family.

It is known that the Chinese have brought in drugs, gotten on the Council of Parliament, and have not been a good influence for Nepal.

Many Chinese came into Nepal, and lady Maoists would go out to the villages and say to others who had not any property, "Let your neighbor put his property into parcels so others can have some." The land was taken whether the landowner wanted to give it to neighbors who had not worked as hard as he.

Chapter Four

Growing Up in Historical Simla, India

After home leave in 1955, my father was posted to Simla, India, less than seventy-five miles from the border of India and Tibet. It was such a fascinating and intense experience of Indian and British history and architecture!

In the lush Himalayan town of Simla, the Sanders family was assigned a twenty-two-room house called Ellerslie Villa, which had been the home of British Colonel Keith Young. The house had the luxury of a tennis court, but no heat.

We lived only in the bottom half. Servants' quarters were on the same level. Having hired help in any country is such a great blessing, what with having to navigate through the local customs and languages. And bazaars!

The US State Department issued us an odd-looking mint-green Willy's Jeep station wagon, which could be used to take family members on personal jaunts as well as to transport Daddy on his field missions to consult with farmers. The Jeep came with a driver who would take my brothers, sister, and me to school in the morning and then take Daddy to local villages near the Tibetan border where he would visit with farmers, whom he gave advice about ways to improve their soils and increase crop production. The driver interpreted for Daddy when there was no one in a particular village who spoke English.

Most villages did have someone who spoke some English. They would rush in to be the interpreter, so they could practice the Queen's language that had been thrust upon them during the British occupation.

Often, Mother would accompany Daddy on a trip down country, just to get a break from the chilly days of Simla, and perhaps to be away from the boredom of the Himalayan beauty.

The Sanders Family 1955
Seated. Left to Right: me, Dad and Mom
Standing Left to Right, Brenda, Craig & Roger

My siblings and I had the choice of going into boarding school or staying in Ellerslie Villa, our home. We chose the latter. My parents hired a teacher from Auckland House School, Miss Adcock, to come and stay in the evenings with us. That provided a bit of cash for the lady, who was on a very small income from the school.

When the British were booted out of India in 1947, many of the Brits stayed on. Most of those who chose to remain, rather than return to England, had either served in the British or Indian Army during the latter part of the century-long British occupation. Many wives of the Army officers had come to India to be near their husbands. When their children were five or six years old, they would be sent by ship from Bombay to relatives in the British Isles to attend school until their parents returned from Asia. Only an English education in a proper boarding school in the "homeland" England or Scotland, would do, don't you know?

During summers in India, these British *memsahibs*, the wives or lady heads of the households, would go up to Simla to get out of the unbearable heat of the plains or the terrai, which was a belt of marshy land at the foot of the Himalayas in northern India.

British-style bungalows, built from local wood and gray or white mountain stone, dotted the tops of the rising hills of Simla. Inside were lovely wood- and glass-paned windows, framed with dusty, faded English fabric. Windows allowed the residents enough light that they could see when they indoors. The windows also allowed them to see out to enjoy, among the morning mists, colorful flowers peeping and creeping among the uneven stones of the walls.

If one were peeking inside from outside, one could see that there was a gray and white stone fireplace with candles on the mantle and a small *vaze*, as the English would say, of colorful mountain wildflowers. The candles were used not just for a bit of romantic decoration, but for lighting, even though of poor quality, when there was no electricity, especially during monsoon season which was accompanied by fog.

Next to the fireplace would be a bit faded and worn overstuffed chair covered in English chintz. On this would be an Afghan throw, knitted out of boredom by the *memsahib*. One could drink only so many G and T's (gin and tonics). And, for that, one must wait until a reasonable hour, so as always to be *proper*. At the appointed, correct hour, all the local foreign gentry would gather at Davie Lal Hall for an evening of tea and cakes or gin and tonics. Posted on the outside of the entry was a sign that said, "No Mad Dogs or Indians Allowed."

Some played snooker. Shouts to the turbaned bearers brought more drinks. Servants pulled ropes to make the large ceiling fans sway in unison. "A little more quickly, please."

"Bloody this" and "Bloody that" and "What the hell is this insurgency all about?" and "Have you heard what Nehru has just done with the Russians?" echoed through Davie Lal Hall.

While all this was going on, my sister and I would sometimes have the rickshaw pullers stop at the club so we could see if any of our friends from another school, Tara Davie, which was Catholic, were in with their parents.

Generally, children were not present, but our stopping by gave us an excuse to observe how the players of the British Raj enjoyed themselves.

Inside the expats' homes were Colonial-style chairs and a three-sided table with a marble top cut from the local quarry. On top of the table, there were piles of books, mostly in English but a few in French, along with customary writing tablets for drafting ones' ever-evolving memoirs.

Rascally flower gardens with low meandering stone fences and walk paths sauntered up and down and around the shortcuts that the locals, including children, took to their rickety tin shacks, most of which had no heat or electricity. These were perched precariously on a piece of rock or tucked in a row of tin along the center of a hill.

On several occasions, we would see a leopard walking back and forth across the edge of our tennis courts, on a hilly ledge down below our house. One evening when we were returning home from a Sunday evening cinema, this leopard (we assumed it was the same one) jumped onto the hood of our Jeep. This was so exciting. We were having an experience that did not surprise us, only a "first" that we had not had before.

Life Is a Stamp Collection

Of course, we children couldn't wait until we procured an aerogramme so we could write home to our friends and to *reassure* our grandparents in the States. It seemed that grandparents were never in favor of the foreign adventure business that the parents assured them was *such good exposure*.

During the following months, we continued to get glimpses of the leopard. One time when my parents were on an agricultural trip down country, we children were "boarding" at our respective schools. When we all eturned home to Ellerslie Villa, we were glad to see each other and be reunited with our German Alsatian dog, Cinders, that had been given to us by Miss Adcock, one of the teaching mistresses at Auckland House School.

After our late dinner, Mother went out to our driveway, which had a steep mountain wall, to place food down for Cinders. Mother then turned, opened the door, and walked inside. As she shut the door, she heard Cinders utter a deep, disturbing growl. Mother glanced outside. Cinders didn't have a chance. Fortunately, the leopard had waited for Mother to leave before he grabbed Cinders.

The next morning, after no sleep and many tears, we each took our wooden walking canes, which we used for traversing the hillsides, to search for Cinders in daylight. We children, trying to comfort our parents as well as ourselves, said, "Maybe the leopard let Cinders go." In the walkway just outside our kitchen, we saw animal feces. Beside a stream just below the servants' quarters, we found grey fur: Cinders' remains.

In the monsoon rainy season there was only an occasional fleeting break in the deluge of torrential rain. At eye level, through dusty school windows, we could see wispy clouds drifting over flowering wild rhododendron trees.

The air was stifling and still. Shrouded in this slow-moving mist, wild orchids hung precariously from host soil, seemingly quite contentedly nestled between broken Himalayan rocks which seemed ready to start a landslide at a moment's notice. An abundance of these families of nature, with mixtures of rhododendrons, orchids, and stones framed in the soil, hung precariously on the steep mountainsides, totally oblivious of their visual gifts. All this melded into the backdrop of the majestic snow-covered mountains, rising as sheer white sheets, outlined by the momentarily emerging blue sky.

In Simla education was quite convenient for our family of four children. I was thirteen. My sister, Brenda, and I attended Auckland House School, which was Canadian. It was very rigid with an intense curriculum. I was in the equivalent of an American seventh grade, although it was called sixth standard.

We also played various sports, which were incorporated into one's regular school day. That concept was new to me. Auckland House was named after Lord Auckland of Boer War fame. And here in Himalayan Simla, it sat on a high knoll.

My brothers—Craig, age ten, and Roger, age six—attended Bishop Cotton School, which was not Anglican, but Catholic. It was the "brother" to Auckland House Girls' School. Again, all classes were taught in English. At Bishop Cotton, young Roger became a big boy, with his gray wool uniform and walking shorts.

The Right Reverend G.E.L. Cotton, Bishop of Calcutta, started the boys' school, as a thanks to God for the deliverance of the British people in India during the Sepoy Mutiny of 1857. It was initially designated "Bishop's School" and came into existence in 1866. It consisted of several detached bungalows in a location given to Rev. Cotton by the Raja of Keonthal. The Governor-General of India, Sir John Lawrence, laid the cornerstone on September 26, 1866. Two weeks later, Rev. Cotton drowned. The name of the institution was changed to Bishop Cotton School.

Craig didn't like the formality of British schools. He would say "Hi" to teachers instead of "Good morning, sir." After one year at that school, he transferred to Woodstock, an up-scale missionary boarding school in Mussoorie, India.

I became well acquainted with the Sundar Singh sisters, who lived in Belvedere House, next to Auckland House. They and their family embraced the Sanders and made us feel welcome to visit them anytime we wished, whether after school or on a weekend.

How nice it was in this foreign land to have quality schools and quality friends. My friend, Rana, reminds me that I used to come running into the house and would call out to her dad, "Hi, Mr. Sundar Singh, how are you?" Indian girls are much more proper. They don't run in the house.

The mountain ridge on which Auckland House sat was usually shrouded in a cloud. I wish I could say it was a misty cloud. The barefoot rickshaw pullers, who took my sister and me to school each morning from our home in Ellerslie Villa, were very deft in not letting us careen off the edge of a cliff as they pulled our rickshaw. Shouts to all who were in the shacks on the slippery hillsides, as well as those in the homes of the elite could be heard through the dense shroud of early morning mist.

On the way to school, we passed near Prime Minister Nehru's home, Wildflower Hall, Vice Regal Lodge, where much of the Pakistan and Indian partition had been planned and pounded out. As we passed, the rickshaw drivers would chant, "*jaya hai, jaya hai, jaya hai!*" to convey "I am here, out of my way; I am here, out of my way!" Onward we went, being tugged and jiggled, through the mountain rain on rickety wooden wheels.

Rudyard Kipling had written about a headless horseman who was frequently seen going through a mountain tunnel in Simla. My sister and I passed through this tunnel each morning on the way to Auckland House. We held our breaths in case the story was true. We never saw this famous figure from Kipling's story, and we felt a little cheated.

Through the gate to Auckland House and up the steep incline to the beautiful old wooden building, the rickshaw bearers struggled to bring us, the *missyshiebs* (young girls). It was never a glorious site, to be there for school. British teaching systems seemed very harsh compared to the leniency of the schools that I had attended in Arkansas. Our teachers, Anglo-Indians and English, were born in India.

One had to stand when the teacher entered, again when asked a question, and then again when the teacher left the room. Whenever an Indian girl did not know the answer to a question, she would burst into tears. I could not get over how much they could cry! However, I could have cried every time I had a new challenge with this school's curriculum. There were about seventeen subjects for us in sixth Standard. I knew Indian and English history and Indian geography so much better than I knew what the surrounding area of Arkansas about my grandparent's home. I missed them dearly.

One of our elderly English class mistresses, Miss Butler, would say, "Oh, cast open the window and breathe in some of that fresh air!" In would roll the fog, but not quite thick enough to hide us from her.

Questions, of course, had to be answered. Our hands in half-fingered mittens were raised high. The mittens were half-fingered so that one could still get one's frozen fingers around a pencil, and I had never seen anything so difficult in my life. What would the British think of next?

So, with fog and frozen fingers, there was no escaping these unfamiliar traditions and rules. There was no such thing as heat in the entire school, except for the Canadian Headmistress's quarters, where there was one fireplace. And one never wanted to be called into her quarters for some type of reprimand, even if warmth were to be a beneficial by-product.

Every morning, we dressed in brown-checked frocks topped by our brown wool school blazers, which had an embroidered crest on the pocket. On this gold and brown crest was embroidered, "Altiora Peto," which means "I seek higher things."

There were collections of students, called *houses*, at Auckland House. Each student belonged to one or the other. My sister belonged to Durant House and wore a green tie. I belonged to Matthew House, which required a yellow tie at the base of the neck of my checked frock. In Arkansas, no one ever dared wear a tie to school, and certainly not a girl!

I had brown shoes, which the school required, which we had made in Hong Kong when our ship had docked there on the way to India. They hurt my feet as I tracked around Auckland House, but they had been especially made for me. I could not waste a good pair of shoes when so many in this country had never even owned a pair.

At Auckland House, I learned to be the lead while dancing the minuet. We had to practice dancing, even though the opposite sexes were not allowed to date, nor would they ever in this "arranged marriage society world." Since I was the tallest, I always had to be the "boy" in learning dances with the other girls. Later, when I was in American high schools, this would inevitably throw me off while being led by boys.

All the girls in Auckland House were from progressive Indian families, whether they were Sikh, Muslim, Hindu, or Christian, who believed in education for females.

A year later, I also transferred to Woodstock to begin my freshman year of high school, so I could get high school credits which could transfer to the States. My youngest brother, Roger, and my sister, Brenda, continued in the English-speaking schools of post-British Simla.

One girl at Auckland House, named Santos Stokes, had an American grandfather, Samuel Evans Stokes, who was born of wealthy parents in Philadelphia, Pennsylvania.

In 1904, Samuel Stokes went to India as a Christian missionary. He lived in a cave while he was administrator of Gorton Mission School in Kotgarh. Soon after his arrival, an earthquake shook the city of Kanga, and Mr. Stokes volunteered to go there to help. Among other duties, he assisted with a cholera epidemic which followed. Subsequently, Stokes assisted with a smallpox epidemic that struck the Indian Punjab, which included Simla.Grandfather Stokes was perhaps best known for having introduced apple production to this section of the Himalayas. He brought seedlings for green apple trees from the US State of Washington and started Golden Delicious apple orchards near Simla. You can see them on the road to the Tibetan border.

At the outbreak of World War I, Stokes joined the British Army. He served as a captain, stationed in India. After the war, he became disillusioned with the British treatment of Indians and served with the India National Congress. In 1919, he began opposition to "beggar caste" forced labor in which some Indian men were forced to carry the baggage for British government officials. Often this posed severe problems for those men who were pulled from their normal work to accommodate the officials. As a "Philadelphia American," Stokes began a letter-writing campaign in Indian newspapers. He also organized protest strikes and public meetings to oppose forced labor.

Mahatma Gandhi took note. He stated in *Young India*: "No Indian is giving such battle to the government as Mr. Stokes."

It was said that Stokes saw neither color nor creed. He married a beautiful Hindu lady. To a large extent because of the work of Samuel Evans Stokes, the practice of disrupting work of the lower caste men was ended. In 1932, Stokes converted to Hinduism from being a Christian missionary.

During World War II, Stokes urged Indian Nationalists to support the British, "not because he thought them admirable, but because he thought the Germans worse."

On May 14, 1946, about nine years before the Sanders family arrived in Simla, Stokes died in Simla's Harmony Hall, which was named after a family residence in New Jersey.

In 1955, Stokes' granddaughter, Santos Stokes, and I were classmates in Auckland House School. She was proud to tell me about her grandfather and the now-famous Golden Delicious apple orchards near Simla.

So here I was, a little girl from Arkansas, attending school with a Royal Rana Princess, Prem, from Nepal, an Indian girl who had American blood from her grandfather, and other very progressive Sikh, Hindu, and Muslim females.

As we walked two-abreast in file from Auckland House to Christ Church on Sunday, three little blond heads—mine and my two siblings—bobbed up and down among the sea of beautiful black-haired Indian students.

In the procession, downhill from the school, across the Hindustan-to-Tibet cart road, and up the mall to Christ Church, usually in monsoon rain, we children sang *Dina Row Your Boat Ashore,* or *Val De Ree Val De Ra,* in our version of harmony. I'm sure the mistress accompanying us was grateful for the hush that we had to observe once inside.

The Anglican music was so different from the Baptist music of Arkansas. To this day, when I hear it, I remember how hauntingly beautiful it was. While sitting in the sanctuary, with no heat, with sunlight coming in through beautiful windows. I didn't realize at the time that they were designed by a famous man in history, Rudyard Kipling. I daydreamed of going home to America. Well, that wasn't about to happen anytime soon.

The Bishop, Reverend Chandra, was Indian. His wife was English. Many years later, I wrote to her after her husband died, asking her if I could interview her for my memoirs. She had moved to Manchester, England, but kept in touch with my mother. I was rather insulted that she did not answer my request directly to me as I thought it was a compliment to her that I found her life interesting. She answered me back through my mother.

I wish now that I had paid more attention to the history of the Simla area, which included "Scandal Point" where two lovers were observed kissing, near the edge of the cliff. In the nineteenth century, it indeed must have been a scandal, since marriages were arranged without the intended couple ever having laid eyes upon each other.

We learned that on May 10, 1857, the Sepoy Mutiny erupted around growing discontent by the Indians with British rule. Apparently, the sepoy, who were Indian soldiers trained by the British, had heard rumors that the cartridges for their new Enfield rifles were greased with lard and beef fat. Because cows are sacred to Hindus and pigs are abhorrent to Muslims, all sepoys were outraged, and they mutinied.

A guide regaled us children with one horrible tale: during one of the charges by the British, at the time of the Sepoy Mutiny, near the famous Red Fort in Old Delhi, someone tricked the British Cavalry into going into a tunnel, where many sepoy had fled. Once the horses and men were deep into the tunnel, the sepoy sealed both ends, leaving the British inside with a tunnel full of cobras. This is one story I wish I could forget.

An ever-present issue was how to deal with the friction between the Muslims and the Hindus. In 1905, Lord Curzon attempted to partition India based on religion. Planning for the proposed split took place in Simla, in Viceregal Lodge and Auckland House (School) which I would later attend, as it became a *mostly* girls' school. Both Muslims and Hindus protested the terms of the proposition.

Some 130 years earlier, British surveyors discovered Simla, a small village tucked away in the Himalayas. Simla seems to have been named after the goddess, Shyamla Devi, an incarnation of the fierce and, frankly, quite frightening-looking Hindu goddess, Kali. They thought it would be an excellent place for the colonizers.

Reports of Simla's climate and its dramatically beautiful surroundings made it grow in popularity. In 1822, civil servant Charles Kennedy built Simla's first British summer home. The village became a resort for British army officers who were recuperating from the Gurkha war. With its few rustic dwellings, Simla lay along the Himalayan ridges at an altitude of a little over 7,000 feet, on the Hindustan-to-Tibet road. For eight months of the year, Simla was the summer capital of the British when they ruled India.

The climate was so much cooler than the usual places where the British had settled down-country. While the soldiers were recuperating, their wives, the *memsahibs,* soon found that Simla was an excellent place to be.

Gradually, the village began to look like a small English countryside. Cottages with gardens, tree-lined walks, churches, and cricket patches came up around town, plus a billiard club or two.

In 1844, the cornerstone was laid for the first Anglican house of worship, Christ Church, where services were held in English. The Right Reverend Thomas Dealtry, Bishop of Madras, consecrated the church in 1857. A century later, my family would worship in this very sanctuary.

Life Is a Stamp Collection

I learned that Lockwood Kipling, the father of my favorite author, Rudyard Kipling, had placed a fresco, which he personally had fashioned, around the chancel window. A clock had been donated to the church by Colonel Dumbleton. In 1873, a porch was added to the edifice.

In 1864, the British formally declared Simla as the summer capital of the Imperial Government. Tons of files and baggage were transported all the way from Calcutta, and later from Delhi to this hill station. Simla seems to have been named after the goddess, Shyamla Devi, who was an incarnation of the fierce and frankly quite frightening looking Hindu goddess, Kali.

Many times, when the monsoons were in full force, bridges would wash out along the Hindustan-to-Tibet Road. Traveling parties, going up to their summer capital, would have to stay by the side of the road while awaiting repairs to a bridge. In those days, in that part of the world, there were no phones.

When a bridge was out, mail to and from Simla would be put on the back of an elephant, which could usually ford the river. However, on a number of occasions, the elephant was not strong enough to cross the currents that had brought down the bridge, so the mail did not get through.

In 1929, the Indian Congress passed "Gandhi's Civil Disobedience Movement." Muslim political leaders, including Pakistani Muhammad Ali Jinnah, and many others, quit Congress in the belief that it was just too dominated by Hindus.

In 1945, I was three years old and living in Arkansas. At that time, Muslims obtained thirty seats in the Legislature, and the Government of India began to plan an interim government. Jinnah of Pakistan and many others saw this as a lessening the power of the Muslims. Lord Mountbatten and his council worked on the details for this in Auckland House.

In 1947, India gained its independence from the British. That same year Pakistan, partitioned from the eastern and western parts of India, was born as a separate Islamic State. In the process, approximately seventeen million Hindus and Muslims were uprooted. Muslims, in what remained as India, moved to the new Pakistan, while Hindus in what became Pakistan moved to India.

During Partition, India and Pakistan disputed the northern portion of old India known as Kashmir, which had a Muslim majority but was controlled by a Hindu Prince. The ensuing violence caused the deaths of some one million people. Trainloads of Muslims from India arrived in Pakistan's train stations with their throats cut. The same happened to Hindus coming out of Pakistan—trainloads of passengers arrived at their destinations with blood spilling from their throats.

My Auckland House boarding school Sikh friends, Rana and Prem Sunder Singh of New Delhi and Simla, told me of some of their returning friends' stories from Pakistan.

While literally walking across the former country, when one of the bad people along the way wanted to kill them, their mother would bribe them with a valuable stone she'd kept tied in the corner of her sari.

After Partition, Muhammad Ali Jinnah became Governor-General of Pakistan. Liaquat Ali Khan was Prime Minister. Soon after Pakistan became a nation, Jinnah died, in 1948.

In India, Jawaharlal Nehru became the first Prime Minister after Partition.

In 1948, a militant Hindu assassinated Mahatma Gandhi, apparently because of his tolerant attitude toward Muslims. Later, one of my classmates at Woodstock, Edith Theilsen, told me that Gandhi's assassination took place very near the Danish Ambassador's residence in New Delhi, where they now lived. Edith's father was the Danish Ambassador.

Five years before the Sanders family arrived in India, Prime Minister Nehru gave his famous "tryst with destiny" speech on August 14, 1947. That speech was beautifully engraved on a large marble stone just outside the Nehru Museum in New Delhi. Twenty-five years later, during a brief visit with my parents, I took a picture of that stone.

In part, this is what it read:

> "Long years ago, we made a tryst with destiny, and now the time comes when we shall redeem our pledge, not wholly or in full measure, but very substantially. At the stroke of the midnight hour, when the world sleeps, India will awake to life and freedom.
>
> A moment comes, which comes but rarely in history, when we step out from the old to the new, when an age ends, and when the soul of the nation, long suppressed, finds utterance. It is fitting that at this solemn moment we take the pledge of dedication to the service of India and her people and to the still larger cause of humanity."

M. Angela Sanders

American boarding school – Woodstock

In 1956, my parents received a letter saying I could start high school in the accredited English-speaking American missionary boarding school, Woodstock.

It is/was located in a distant area in the Himalayan Mountains. Woodstock had been established in 1854 by Mennonites and Presbyterians. It coincided with the dominance of the East India Company. Though the school was managed by the Americans during the Raj, at times it provided refuge for families who opposed British rule in India.

This was going to be a terrific new beginning for me!

So, in 1957, I started my freshman high school year in this American curriculum boarding high school located in Mussoorie, India. We traveled on sooty Indian trains, changing trains occasionally, and climbed and climbed until we finally reached the hill-station in Mussoorie.

The students were mainly Americans from Foreign Service families living in neighboring countries, and US lifelong missionary families of different Christian faiths. There were also children of United Nations families plus a few Hindus, Muslims, and Sikhs.

One of my American classmates, Penny Shoemaker, came in from Indonesia, the largest Muslim country. Her parents were Methodist missionaries there.

The furniture in my room at Woodstock was sparse and rickety. The floor was concrete. A window with no curtains allowed the drafty cold mountain air to creep inside. If I wanted to be warm, I had to sit inside a momentary ray of sunshine washing through the window.

Back home in Simla, I was accustomed to US State Department's Danish Modern furniture. I called the dorm mother for girl students and explained, "I need a better bureau. This one is falling apart!"

She probably chuckled to herself. The furniture was not changed. I soon learned that all the other rooms had the same misshapen sorts of pieces.

Life Is a Stamp Collection

There was a lovely Anglo-Indian lady, Miss Marley, who had been there for quite a few years. She was born to George and Margaret Sinclair when her mother was eighteen and her father was twenty-five. She had four siblings. Her father was inducted into "Courage with Humanity" Masonic Lodge in Calcutta on Feb. 13, 1902. The reason I mention this, is that my father was inducted into the Masonic Lodge in the States, in the late 1940s.

The capitol of British India used to be Calcutta but was moved to Delhi in 1911. Simla was the summer capital, and the *sahibs* and *memsahibs* would go there for the summer, and this is where we Sanders were posted in 1955, less than seventy-five miles from the Tibet/ Indian border.

Back to Woodstock, my roommate, Francie Gonzales, was from another State Department family, from New Mexico. I had never known anyone from New Mexico or anyone by the name of Gonzales.

Francie was an only child whose parents were based in New Delhi. She soon became the most popular student. She had a beautiful smile and exuded kindness. We walked to class together and giggled when American fellows would do a wolf whistle and shout from below on the mountainside, "Hey, Francie, look at me. I'm about to fall over into the *khud!*" (*Khud* is a Hindi word meaning down the mountainside.)

Francie and I were in school plays together. We had a great group of girlfriends from State Department and missionary families.

One day as I walked down one of the steep hills from class, toward our dorm, a black car sat outside the entryway. As I approached our dorm, I saw Francie inside, crying. She rolled down the window and, as she sobbed, told me that her father had suffered a heart attack. As the only child, her mother wanted her to return home to Delhi immediately. The car had been sent from Delhi to take her to her parents. My best and first American friend in many years was now leaving me, in her sadness. I would now start anew amid the cliques of born-in-India missionary kids. They were a group who were very self-assured and secure and spoke several local languages. You had to admire that.

My new roommate was an upperclassman, Maudie Lee Brookshire. She was also from a US State Department family. Her parents' home was in the Helmand Valley of Afghanistan where, like I, Maudie had been homeschooled with the Calvert system.

Maudie was a free spirit. This may be one reason her parents sent her to Woodstock. With her, she said, a little bit of missionary could go a long way.

Maudie was one of the few in school who dated openly. Indian society did not condone dating by young people, but here in our somewhat closed environment at Woodstock, a few progressive students did.

Many years later, Maudie Lee surprised me pleasantly when she and her husband, John Davis, visited me in Florida.

When my father's tenure in the Foreign Service in Simla ended, my Woodstock days came to an end. From Woodstock in Mussoorie and from Ellerslie Villa in Simla, the Sanders family moved back to the USA to the beautiful Ozark Mountain town of Huntsville, Arkansas. President Eisenhower was now in office. Under him, the Foreign Service Food Development program remained a high priority. It had as well under the Democrats when they were in office. Hunger knows no favorites or political parties. Everyone would do well to please remember that.

In 1988 or so, as I was in the process of moving to Marco Island in Florida, I learned that the minister of the Presbyterian Church there, Reverend Bruce Fiol, had also attended Woodstock. Some of his brothers had been my schoolmates thirty years earlier in Mussoorie, India.

Chapter Five

High School and College in Arkansas

In 1957, when I was fifteen, after the majestic beauty of Simla and the surrounding Indian and Tibetan Himalayas, the Sanders family was posted to another mountainous range called the Ozarks. In Huntsville, Arkansas. I would start tenth grade in an American school!

We seemed to fit right in with most Huntsville families, whose ancestors also had come from Scotland, Germany, or Italy with perhaps a small amount of American Indian blood intermixed. Their homes were nestled up, down, and around, on pine-tree laden hillsides. When there was no breeze, the houses looked at various times of day as if they were ducking in and out of the summer sun's hot, shifting, dusty rays.

Dairy cows, grazing in lush, verdant pastures, knew to go to shade trees when their bull lay quietly under an old oak. To add to the exquisite Arkansas beauty, long necked pine trees graced the rising hills of the Ozarks. Pine trees later figured into our future. My father bought tracts of forestry land, which I managed as a business for my sister and brothers after Daddy died.

Nestled in the Ozark Mountains in Madison County of northwestern Arkansas, Huntsville is both picturesque and laid-back. During summer, the sun beat down relentlessly. The gentle breezes scarcely stirred a leaf.

School was a bit of an adjustment for me. Students with whom I made friends in the sophomore year of high school had not been exposed to foreign-service life. They would talk about how, on their summer vacations, they had helped build a barn, and that was why they had a tan. When I shared my experience the previous year of riding an elephant in Bratnager, India, they would gasp and say, "Oh, that is just too wild to believe." I soon learned to keep those stories to myself. It seemed to me that my classmates were perfectly willing not to be curious. Sometimes I envied that they had a contentment that I missed. I was always so curious, wanting to know more and more.

Arkansas's famous Governor Orval Faubus, together with his wife Alta and son Farrell, lived in our little county-seat town of Huntsville. In 1954, the Supreme Court had established the rule for the entire United States. Only the states of Virginia and Arkansas defied the edict. Governor Faubus made headlines by defying Federal orders to integrate the Arkansas school system. He stood up to President Eisenhower and closed the schools so that blacks could not attend and be integrated.

Eventually, of course, Eisenhower won, and the schools stayed open in Little Rock. President Eisenhower ordered Federal troops into Little Rock, our state's capital, to oversee the rights and safety of black children in school. These minority students were finally being given the opportunity for an equal education, through integration. Eleven hundred troops of the 101st Airborne Division arrived in the state capital. Their mission was to escort Minniejean Brown, a young black girl, and eight other black children, to enroll in an all-white school, the now-famous Little Rock Central High School.

On September 17, 1957, with the press with their cameras and the public anxiously watching, Governor Faubus had to acquiesce. Minniejean Brown made history, moving our state and nation toward a new era of intended equality.

The Sanders family were neighbors of the Faubus family. Because we had arrived in Huntsville with no household goods, my parents set out to acquire furniture for our family of six. Mother went to estate sales, where she often found Alta Faubus, the Governor's wife, seeking antiques. The Sanders family still has an old Lincoln-style bed of exquisite dark wood for which Mother outbid Mrs. Faubus.

The picturesque and small hamlet of Huntsville had approximately 1,500 people, being mostly farmers. Some also had businesses around the old western-style town square.

As a teenager new to America, I learned that "draggin' Main" meant driving around and around this town square in late evening.

If one had already seen the weekly movie at the local movie house, going into Fayetteville to attend an event at the University of Arkansas was another option. Fayetteville was only thirty minutes away.

One of my friends whose father would let her have the family car for an evening would sometimes call. She would pick up several of us at our homes and off we would go to the local Dairy Queen. After a milkshake, we would wait the customary, sufficient length of time, then slowly back out of the parking lot while carefully dodging carhops clad in the short-shorts and white sleek-bladed roller skates. We were on an unstated mission, but on a definite charted course, in which we pretended not to see anyone—like good-looking local fellows—who for sure were eyeing us. With windows rolled down and the car moving just slowly enough so as not to do an embarrassing stall, which would have precipitated a "clutch pop," we would circle the square. Only guys in duck tails and crew tops did clutch pops, to let girls know they were around.

While we pretended to be oblivious to honks, catcalls, and waves, our car gently moved forward with windows down so the breeze barely moved our hair.

These young Arkansas farmers' sons with farmer tans, were in pickup trucks and low-slung, late-model Ford and Mercury convertibles.

Farming and store businesses apparently were profitable in this Huntsville area. So, around and around we went, passing White Castle Café, Phillips Dry Cleaners and Saddle Repair, Cogers' Ladies Ready to Wear, and Piggly Wiggly Grocery Store.

On the downside, as Huntsville lies directly on the Trail of Tears, we of course were always surrounded by the colorful and sad history of the Osage and Cherokee Tribes, which had been there long before we palefaces arrived.

In the 1700s, the Osage Indians lived in Missouri, and they claimed this corner of what became Arkansas as their hunting ground. In the modern era of 1957, the area now housed Huntsville.

The Osage were tall and of a warlike nature. Later, the Cherokee were moved out of east Tennessee and Georgia. The relocation of the Cherokee was a horrid affair. Many moved to Arkansas on their own and lived there relatively peacefully until about 1829 when they were pushed further into Indian Territory in what became the State of Oklahoma in 1904.

Their time in the Huntsville area was short by history's timetable. They had been in this area from 1780 to 1830, and now my own nomadic family was living in a town which lay amongst their trails sprinkled with arrowheads which had become lost in the brush. Still visible though, along certain trails, were bent-over trees that had been used by the Indians to dry wild-animal hides. By 1780, the "Old Settler" Cherokees had taken up white man's dress, farming, and trade systems.

As a young granddaughter, I occasionally spent summers in Mena, my grandparents' hometown. One-time, Aunt Madge, and her grandson, Gary, who was about my age, came to visit us in Mena. They accompanied us in my grandfather's Model T Ford to a heavily forested area with many different types of trees present there since the Indians had inhabited that part of Arkansas.

Gary and I got up very early and left the cabin to hunt for snake skins and other unique treasures. Indians had left arrowheads behind. When I found more treasures than Gary did, it really made my day! While others were sleeping, we found and placed our snake skins around the leg of a dining table. Then we waited impatiently outside until one of our grandmothers let out a shrill shriek. We got the perfect response from our grandmothers: curiosity. How could it have gotten there? Those were wonderful times—to be in nature and get a sense of that not-so-long-ago Indian history!

Mena had an interesting beginning, with the Kansas City, Pittsburg, and Gulf Railroad running through it. Financing of the railroad was provided by the Netherlands, which precipitated gratitude from the local settlers. They named the town after Queen Wilhelmina of Holland. Wilhelmina was born in 1880 and died in 1964. She became heir presumptive after her half-brother died when she was seven years old. So, there was history for naming the town after Dutch royalty.

The small hamlet of Mena sits nestled in the Ouachita Mountains. The nearest towns are Ft. Smith, Arkansas, and Texarkana, Texas.

Today, there is a hotel named the Queen Wilhelmina Inn, which sits on a high ridge of the Ouachita Mountains. Because it sits on the historic route of the old stagecoach outside of Mena, its history breathes of memories of toil, struggle, Indian fights defending its lands with the white man, and quiet resolute beauty. It doesn't need to speak; it stands there as its own monument to us all, "with a wonderful view of so much of God's glory."

My maternal grandfather, Silas Ervin Craig, whose family hailed from Scotland, was a very kind and generous man. When he saw my grandmother, Pearlee Stanley, he immediately wanted to court her, as they said back then. In order to buy her an engagement ring, he added extra felled lumber to the horse wagons so that he could save money to be able to ask Pearlee to marry him. When he worked up the nerve to ask her to marry him, they kissed for the first time. My grandmother worried while walking all the way home that she would become pregnant. The facts of life were not discussed openly back then. So, Silas Ervin Craig was then engaged to Pearlee Stanley who would soon become Pearl Craig!

My maternal grandmother's family, the Stanley family, moved by covered wagon to settle in Boardcamp, outside of

Mena, Arkansas, in 1900. After my grandparents were married, my grandfather purchased a rock lodge which sat in a cleared area of the Ouachita Mountains, some distance from the old stagecoach town of Mena.

Just a short side note, jumping ahead to 2010: One day I was on a country-side tour in Scotland, and we were by Balmoral Castle. The tour director said that because Queen Elizabeth was in residence he could only point out various features as she did not like the noise of buses stopping and starting. At that precise time, I turned to look at the opposite side of the road and there in view was a small sign that said "Craig" with an arrow pointing down a small country lane. If my grandfather's family was from there exactly, I will never know, but what a lovely thoughtful gift from the Divine.

Prairies stretch across much of Oklahoma, but the state also holds mountain ranges, including the Ouachita Mountains in the southeastern corner. Formed over 300 million years ago, these mountains are a highly eroded remnant of a much larger range, one that may have stretched from Texas into southeastern Canada.

The Ouachita Mountains record a complicated geologic history spanning hundreds of millions of years. Long before the first dinosaur evolved, what is now the southern central United States sat at the bottom of an ancient sea. From roughly 340 to 550 million years ago, the area collected sediments eroding off nearby continents as well as detritus of sea life.

Starting around 340 million years ago, a tectonic plate that had previously been attached to Africa and South America collided with the North American Plate. The process helped form the supercontinent of Pangaea and thrust the ancient sea floor skyward. The similarities between rock layers of the Ouachita Mountains and the Appalachian Mountains indicate that they were part of a massive mountain chain formed by this collision. Once elevated, the mountains soon commenced eroding.

Life Is a Stamp Collection

About 200 million years ago, Pangaea began to break apart. The breakup wrenched apart the supersized mountain range, leaving a wide swath of low-lying land between the Ouachita Mountains in the west and the Appalachian Mountains in the east. A low-profile land persists today across the southern US.

One time I had a date with Farrell Faubus, who was overweight, drove a Corvette, and drank Old Crow from a bottle he stowed under the front seat. As a fifteen-year-old, I was all eyes, as dating was something new to me. Farrell eventually married a beautiful redhead, Martha Jo Culwell, from Huntsville High School class of 1960. After a few years, the couple divorced. Farrell later committed suicide.

I had experienced so much by the time I was ready to date that my intuition was thrown off balance. I had met so many varied people, from rajas to lepers, from ambassadors to kings, so small-town boys didn't impress me much. I knew I was to go to college, and that ambition had to come before I could even think of a serious relationship. I didn't know what to look for in a boyfriend, so if he went to the Baptist church, that seemed okay with my parents for me to date him.

As a teenager, I sometimes helped my friend, Patsy, on her dad's dairy farm, which was near where I lived. We would drive a topless Jeep in the sunset of the cool of the evening, over the hilly land to round up the dairy cows and herd them back to the milking barn. The Jeep had no brakes, but this didn't seem to bother me or Patsy. We would skid around in a circle at the base of the hill near the barn and come to a thankful stop. Of course, this generated tons of dust.

On Saturdays, Patsy's dad would pay us to scrub fly specks off the milking equipment and the ceiling, before "inspections."

In 1957, I had my first boyfriend, Winford Philips, age nineteen. I was fifteen. He worked at Oklahoma Tire and Supply and was a handsome fellow, a dark-tanned Huntsville High

School grad. He was one-quarter Cherokee Indian. His father owned a butcher shop; his mother was a Pentecostal preacher.

While I lived in Huntsville, we dated until Winford met a beautiful brunette who was crowned "Miss Springdale Rodeo Queen" in the next county. And then, he dated "Miss Oklahoma Rodeo Queen" who was visiting. Winford and I dated a bit after that, but I learned a life-long lesson. Your heart never heals after deception by your first love. We were exclusive, but that mattered not.

At any rate, Winford enlisted in the military, and our family moved to Batesville, Arkansas, nestled on the White River, where I spent my senior year and graduated from high school.

Winford was a captain with the Arkansas State Police for many years, until he retired to his hobby farm just outside of Huntsville to tend to his Texas Longhorn cattle.

In 2005, I sent Winford a note on Classmates.com. In his response, he reminded me that we had dated again when I attended the University of Arkansas in 1962. I hadn't remembered that. He talked with pride about his three children. Finally, he said, "We should have a way to let each other know if one of us dies. I have told my oldest son about you. I have remained in love with you all these years."

I called Winford in 2007: "Might you and your wife meet with my sister Brenda and me when we attend Huntsville High School Reunion this coming August?"

He said, "I can't talk. Could I call you back a little later?" When he returned the call, he said, "Guess where I was when you called. I received a call from Governor Mike Beebe to come and talk with him regarding a new security task force for Arkansas. He wants me to come out of retirement and head it up!" Winford added, "I will see about attending the forty-seventh high school reunion."

That reunion was a first for me. I had not graduated from there, because my parents had moved, and I had spent my senior year at another school.

But, after all, he was still in love with me, and I had invited his wife as well. Right? He never showed and never explained his absence.

I graduated from high school in Batesville three years after arriving back from India. In 1960, I attended Arkansas State College for my freshman year of college. This was about an hour from the Mississippi River. At Arkansas State, I had a nice group of female and male friends from the town of Batesville.

While attending Arkansas State University, in the college town of Jonesboro, some of the fellows proposed that we drive to Memphis, Tennessee, just across the Mississippi River, some Saturday evening and go to a blues bar. I had my very first drink of alcohol, a typical southern college town tradition of bourbon and Coke.

As we were there in this lazy, smoky blues bar, Rowena Carter, a girl from another table, asked if I was Angela Sanders. She had overheard someone say my name. It turns out that we had been neighbors and best friends in Paragould, Arkansas in 1947 when we both were five years old. It was now 1961. We didn't get to talk, as our respective groups were noisy, the music was loud, and the bourbon tasted awful.

The next year I transferred to the University of Arkansas in Fayetteville for my sophomore and junior years. By 1962, I returned to the area of the long-gone Osage Indians, Huntsville, which was thirty miles from Fayetteville, and the area where my very first boyfriend, Winford Phillips had lived.

In the 1990s, I read in *USA Today* that many people, including some scientists and actors, who had been in the Nevada Desert during the 1950s when atomic testing was going on had died of cancer. During that time, the wind drifted over several states, carrying the toxic radiation with it. Lo and behold, Madison County, Arkansas, where I had breathed in the dust and drank the milk of the dairy cows, was listed as one of the fateful counties. I wonder if my time in Madison County could be related to health problems I experienced years later? A thyroid cancer removed in 1964, a brain tumor (melanoma) removed in 1996, and another brain tumor removed in 2003?

Chapter Six

Walking Across Oceans
(1963 – 2003)

"... for decades, airlines in America and elsewhere used carefully selected, perfectly groomed young women to persuade their mainly male customers that sitting in cramped aluminum tins for hours at a stretch was a pleasurable experience.... (Stewardesses) had to leave their jobs once they married, were often subject to snap underwear inspections, and had to retire at 32."

– *The Economist*, in a May 5, 2007, review of Kathleen Barry's book, **Femininity in Flight**.

High Heels, Girdles and Gloves

I went for an interview with an American Airlines recruiter. Twice. I wanted to be one of the "one in two hundred" who was interviewed and accepted to become a stewardess. Then I waited, less-than-patiently, for the results. Finally, my dream came true. I just about died. Really. I received the acceptance letter inviting me to begin the rigorous training program.

For six grueling weeks, I stayed up late at night studying for FAA exams, trying to lose weight to maintain a practically-anorexic look, and jumping down slides emulating emergency evacuation situations.

On September 18, 1963, I graduated from American Airlines Stewardess College in Fort Worth, Texas, and received my Wings. Mother and my two Texas aunts attended the graduation ceremony. My father was in Thailand on his new assignment with the United States Operations Mission, the successor to President Truman's Point Four program.-

My Graduation

Late in the afternoon of graduation day, I was on a jet to LaGuardia Airport, where I had been assigned for my first domicile. I'd be based out of LaGuardia while living in Manhattan. What a wonderful new opportunity. I soon fell in love with the excitement and energy of New York City.

Training classes at LaGuardia were primarily for the specific aircraft that were flown up and down the East Coast: Convair 240, Convair 990, DC7s and DC6s. In November, I was assigned "Reserve."

On November 22, 1963, I was on my way from my apartment to LaGuardia to pick up some papers when I heard the news: President Kennedy had been shot! That evening, after returning to my apartment, I awaited a call from Crew Schedule to give me my Reserve assignment for the following day. When the call came, I told the scheduler, "Anyplace but Dallas!" Guess what. I was assigned to Dallas's Love Field on a "707 extra section," to bring out reporters and other passengers. Bright and early on November 23, I deadheaded to Love Field. *Deadheaded* meant the flight had no passengers aboard.

On boarding in Dallas, when the last passenger entered the plane, the doors closed. With that, we fellow travelers started a new chapter in our individual and collective lives as Americans, embarking on an unintended, unplanned emotional national path. As the 707 became airborne, banked to the side, and then continued up and over Dallas, I sat stunned by the events that I was so close to. Our President had just been in this city and, here, our President had been assassinated by an American from Ft. Worth. Our young President had arrived on Air Force One, vibrant and alive to the duties to his nation. Now, Air Force One had departed Dallas with his body and his widow.

Being with these special passengers now, who only a few hours ago had heard the news of the arrival of the President and who had witnessed the parade, fostered a connection like no one ever, ever, anticipated. As I walked through the first class cabin, some people were quietly looking out their windows with no visible emotions. Others, men and women alike, had tears gently rolling down their cheeks. I consciously avoided intruding into their grief, but if I could catch their eye, I would indicate that I would like to bring them a beverage, a meal, a magazine, or a blanket as salve for their pain—anything to assuage what we all felt.

No one wanted anything. They just wanted not to have to believe what they knew was true.

Visiting Parents in Thailand

In 1964, I took my very first vacation trip since I had joined American Airlines and went to Thailand. My family was living in Bangkok, where my father was stationed with the US Overseas Mission. On the first leg of the trip, I flew from Dallas to Honolulu on Pan American Airlines. This would be my first time to see the American flag illuminated on the tail of a Pan Am plane since traveling as a child on the return trip from New Delhi to the States. In those days, seeing the American flag on a plane always brought visions of grandparents and hamburgers and soon-to-be-on-American-soil in Arkansas! Even if the plane did depart at 4:30 a.m.

As we landed in beautiful Hawaii, I immediately fell in love with its seductive beauty. But before I could relax and enjoy the scenery, I went to the consulates of a few of the countries where we would be stopping en route to Thailand, to obtain visas for those countries, in case I got bumped. Airline people nearly always traveled standby because we were offered large standby discounts.

With that chore behind me, I went to the beach to try to learn to surf. On that first afternoon, I rented a surfboard and walked to the edge of the water. This was going to be a piece of cake. Gorgeous, gorgeous, peaceful waves. As I paddled against the waves and gulped the saltwater slapping against my face, I thought I was going down for the third time when suddenly the head of a most handsome fellow bobbed up near mine.

He said, "Could I teach you how to surf?"

In my bit of an Arkansas drawl, I said, "Y-y-yes."

It turned out that this handsome guy was a military man

stationed in Thailand; he was on R & R in Hawaii. I'm sure he was an excellent teacher, although I never quite got the hang of the "hang 10." But I agreed to meet him for a sight-seeing tour and dinner that evening. He was a perfect gentleman. We rode for miles in a convertible sports car around an island that, to this day, I never tire of visiting.

He and some other military fellows were on the same Pan Am flight with me the next day, from Honolulu to Bangkok. When we landed in Bangkok, a vehicle was waiting for the military men. My family, who were supposed to meet me at 3:00 a.m., were nowhere to be seen. I would learn later that Roger, my youngest brother, had failed to set the alarm correctly. He has a very high IQ, but sometimes it fails him ...

Once again, the handsome military fellows came to my rescue. They gave me a ride into Bangkok, through the most exotic looking neighborhoods and on to my family's street and inside their compound.

Guess what? My family was not there. They were headed at breakneck speed for the airport. We must have passed each other along the way as my parents were fussing at Roger for his poor alarm-setting skills!

The gatekeeper graciously admitted us into the yard of my parents' home and the lady servant let me into the house, as I suppose I looked like I belonged to this funny-looking Caucasian family.

My family soon arrived back from the airport. Before the military men left, they asked if I might like to get together with them Sunday evening. I said I would get back to them.

I would have been delighted, but Mother told me that the foreign missionary community church had just acquired a new piano. No one in the small congregation knew how to play it. Mother said, "We would just love it if you could come and play for all the local missionaries as well as some Foreign Service people who will be at the church service Sunday evening."

I could not refuse Mother, so I had to say "no" to those great gentlemen. And that was the only time that they would be free before reporting for duty. Sadly, our paths never crossed again.

Life Is a Stamp Collection

My parents were eager to talk. They explained that in the morning there would be a slight jingle on the telephone. My mother said, as a joke, that we would then be on NBC. In other words, the story was that a CIA agent had lived in this house before he was transferred out of Thailand. The phone tapping agency apparently thought that my father was also CIA.

Finally, as our excitement wore down, I was allowed to go to bed and sleep for about thirteen hours. I was drained. Sitting on a plane as a passenger is exhausting!

The next day, I noticed that the family home was on the front side of a klong, which seems to be quite usual in Thailand. This is a narrow, or sometimes not-so-narrow water transportation system all around and through Bangkok.

That Sunday evening, I played the piano for the wonderful people who were very altruistic in wanting to help those who did not have the fine luck of being born in a developed nation.

While visiting my parents in Bangkok, I heard about the legend of Jim Thompson, who was called the Thai Silk King. Thompson worked for *Vogue* in New York. He helped bring notoriety to Thai silk, which until then had not been effectively merchandised internationally. The story goes that Jim Thompson was later kidnapped, reportedly by the Chinese, who wanted expert advice on getting their international trade developed for silk. He was upcountry visiting friends for the weekend. One afternoon, he went to retire to his rooms; a struggle was heard outside on the gravel drive; he was never seen again in Thailand.

With gift money from our father, Brenda and I bought some Jim Thompson silk at his local shop in Bangkok. In a nearby shop, we had dresses tailored a la Jackie Kennedy style!

Once, when my parents were to return to Bangkok from being on home leave, I took them to the Dallas/Fort Worth airport for departure. As we awaited departure time in an airport restaurant, Mother said, "You know that feeling when you are about to see someone you know?" Hmmm ...

About that time, an American missionary lady from Thailand walked toward us. Mother and she had quite the conversation. Somehow, the subject turned to Jim Thompson. Each wanted to know if the other knew anything further about his disappearance. The missionary lady said that another missionary friend of hers had recently been in Hong Kong. As she walked up the street, on the Kowloon side, Jim Thompson came walking toward her, flanked by two Chinese men. The lady got a clear signal from Thompson, who knew her, not to acknowledge him. An interesting bit of lore. I don't believe that they ever knew for sure about his disappearance.

During my time in Bangkok, I met many of my parents' friends at a lovely party in my honor. International friends and Americans alike, living abroad, generally forge quite a bond, and lasting friendships are cemented. I felt so fortunate to meet these interesting people, friends of my parents.

On my trip to Bangkok from the States, I brought a bundle of gifts: mostly lingerie and makeup. My friend, Harvey Berkowitz, who worked for Kaiser Roth in New York, had given me these things for my mother and her friends. Mother felt that it would not be right for her to have received so many pretty things without sharing. She knew how much it would mean to other ladies, especially missionaries for whom it was nearly impossible to import such luxurious items. So, she gave many of her lady friends, missionaries, and United Nations ladies alike, some of the frilly and pretty things.

Brenda & I with sleeping Buddhist nun

Soon, my month was up, and it was time for me to say my goodbyes and return to flying out of Dallas. I was so fortunate to have seen Bangkok, my family, and their many international friends.

Bill Cherry and Eddie Rickenbacker

During the mid-to-late 1960s, I flew several times out of Amon Carter Field in Ft. Worth with American Airlines Captain Bill Cherry. He was special. My friend Marilyn Eacker, an international flight attendant with American Airlines, was Bill Cherry's love for about thirty-five years, before he died a few years ago with congestive heart failure.

Perhaps some of the older readers of this story will remember Bill Cherry as the pilot of the B-17 plane that in the autumn of 1942 was transporting 52-year-old Captain Edward "Eddie" Rickenbacker. Eddie R. was a top US flying ace in World War II, on a special mission in the Pacific for the Secretary of War, during World War II. Due to faulty navigational equipment, the crew became lost, and the plane ran out of fuel. Cherry did a successful landing in the ocean. They all promptly abandoned the plane; minutes later it sank.

Except for one person, they survived the harrowing twenty-three-day ordeal before being rescued. Cherry was spotted first and rescued. He then directed Navy planes to rescue Rickenbacker the next day.

Marilyn wrote some facts down and sent them to me via e-mail in 2007. She stated. "The First Commando Group was the forerunner to the Green Berets. After Bill was picked up in the Pacific with Rickenbacker, he was shipped off to India with a group of handpicked pilots and other Air Force personnel."

Bill was the commanding officer of the C-47 pilot group that towed the first gliders behind enemy lines in Burma.

The First Commando Group was headed by General Charles Russhon Chenault, General Wingate from Great Britton, The Chindets from China, Colonel Phil Cochran, Colonel John Allison (now General John Allison.)

Much has been written about the First Commando Group, and Milton Caniff wrote a daily comic in the papers named "Steve Canyon" and "Terry and The Pirates," about the group.

In my early days of being a flight attendant, I worked trips with this fast-talking Southern- drawling Bill Cherry. I liked him and thought he was quite a fun character. And he landed our aircraft "just fine."

Chapter Seven

My Marriage to Dr. Al Edinger

After graduating from stewardess college and being based in New York for about thirteen months, I decided it was time to explore and experience the '60s in California. I had no idea that the '60s would unfold as they did!

In 1965, my roommate in New York, Joanie Kranik, found the courage to leave the never-sleeping island of Manhattan and move to Manhattan Beach, California, a suburb of Los Angeles. She told me how exciting it was. So, I put in for a base transfer to Los Angeles.

The transfer didn't come through, and it didn't come through, and it didn't come through. I kept asking my supervisor, "Is my transfer to LAX here yet?"

The answer was always, "No. No. No."

Then I visited a friend in San Francisco whom I had met when she was working temporarily for a New York travel agency. I decided that my destiny would be to go to San Francisco. It felt just phenomenal to be in that city's energy. I totally fell in love with it.

I quietly made plans, mentally, on which hill I would live. Then I got a call from my supervisor who said that my transfer had come through. I was so excited until I was told it was for Los Angeles, not San Francisco. Oh, no!

There was no way I could rescind my LAX transfer; that was the airline's rule. I was heartbroken. American Airlines said if I would go to LAX and stay for the required six months, then I could put in a new transfer order for SFO.

I packed up my New York apartment. A fellow next door drove me, along with a hefty number of boxes marked "stand-by shipment," to La Guardia.

When I arrived at LAX, Joanie and her new fellow, Ron, picked me up along with the boxes of my possessions. I was to live on the third floor with them in an A-frame house on the beach.

This house was just a few steps up from the sand and the rolling waves of the Pacific Ocean in Manhattan Beach. Oh, how one could smell that wonderful, salty, sunshiny air. Would a bikini be in my future?

I became enchanted with Los Angeles. And Joanie and Ron were the perfect couple in love. They talked to me about their "jazzy" doctor friend. Joanie repeatedly said to me, "I wish you could meet him. He's really nice, he's single, and he's handsome! He drives sports cars, and sometimes he even races them up in Riverside. Somehow we must get you two to meet."

Soon, I was invited to go along with the three of them to a sports racing event on a sunny Sunday afternoon. I called in sick for a trip that I was to work that weekend. When my supervisor mentioned my "sick record" shortly thereafter, at my periodic personnel review, I was a little bit indignant.

We caravanned to the racetrack. I rode with Dr. Edinger in his fantastic Corvette. He was everything Joanie had said he was. He was tanned and handsome. He had a funny sense of humor that can hit you with a bit of a chuckle and then with great laughter. He appeared to be a man of great depth and was a keen conversationalist.

But, after that first date, I did not hear from him as it seemed he had a beautiful brunette girlfriend named Dee. She looked like a young Jill St. John, and she drove one of those newly released Ford Mustangs designed by Lee Iacocca. How could I top that, with my second-hand red convertible Sunbeam? I decided that this Dr. Edinger would not be in my life. That was just the way it was to be.

San Francisco faded more and more in my thoughts. Then one day when I needed a medical prescription and was enroute to work a trip out of LAX to Dulles Field in Washington, DC, I stopped by to ask Dr. Edinger's nurse to help me. As I spoke to her, dressed in my summer light pale blue uniform with its little pill box hat, which just happened to match my blue eyes perfectly, Dr. Edinger came into the waiting room. He said, "Hi, Ange, how are you, and where are you off to?"

I said, "I'm on my way to work a 707 flight to Washington, and I just stopped by to see if you might write me a thyroid prescription."

"Sure. By the way, when you return in a couple of days, would you like to go out that evening?"

There really was a God. Dr. Edinger had asked me out, right in front of his office staff, patients, and God!

I floated all the way to Washington's Dulles Field with my head in the clouds. And I was working with some close friends with whom I could share my news: I was to have a date with Al Edinger!

The following poem captures my feeling on that flight:
I am knee deep in clouds,
I am one with the sky, since your heart
made my heart want to fly.
(Author unknown)

At the end of that working trip, I drove home to Manhattan Beach. The excitement was overwhelming. If only that same kind of feeling could prevail for us throughout our lives. The feeling was even better than my looking forward to those Popsicles on the Missouri side of the river, on those hot summer Sunday afternoons during my childhood in Arkansas.

In short, Al and I fell in love. It was a whirlwind courtship and a fairytale proposal. In 1967, husband-to-be, Albert Gustav Edinger, Jr., M.D., and I wanted to be married in the romantic month of February. It is the birthday month for me as well as for my oldest brother Craig, and it also had the distinction of being my parents' wedding month. Not to mention Valentine's Day.

I continued to work as an airline stewardess, as we were called in those days. Our company, AAL. Rules in my company for stewardesses were: *no* marriage was allowed, and I must resign at the age of thirty-two. I was twenty-five. I wanted to be married to Al, but I had to keep the marriage a secret from the airlines. Since this was common practice among stewardesses, I was not alone in breaking the rule.

Al and I had been living together in a rented apartment in Torrance, California. When we returned from Mexico, we planned to move into his beautiful home on the Palos Verdes hillside after I had it redecorated. His *ex-girlfriend*, Audrey, had recently moved out to marry a wealthy Arizona businessman who was with the McCulloch Corporation, the company that successfully reassembled the famously purchased London Bridge in Lake Havasu.

The plan was to be married in Guadalajara, Mexico, on February 28, 1967. On the night prior to our departure for Mexico, I received a phone call from a man who asked me if I was aware that Al was having an affair with his wife, who was one of Al's patients. He asked me if I knew that my intended husband had two children from a marriage when he was in medical school, before his marriage to Audrey.

Of course, I didn't. "That can't be true," I said. "Al and I are leaving for Guadalajara in the morning to be married."

"Yes, I know," he said. "That's why I am calling. I think you should know what you are really getting into."

With this bombardment of what I was sure was false information, I stoically defended Al. When he came home that evening, I was terribly nervous, but calm, as I sought an explanation.

As usual, he was very adept at convincing me that all was untrue, that truly I was the only and greatest love of his life. He cried and threw his glasses across the floor for emphasis. He sobbed and begged that I should not believe all this man had said, but yes, he did have two children from his first marriage to Ruth. The man who subsequently married Ruth after Al left had adopted his two children. It never occurred to me that a parent could just walk away from his own babies and not tell the person he loved—me, in this case—about it.

Still, I was comforted by Al's explanations. As far as he was concerned, there had only been that common transference of feelings between a patient and a caring physician. No true love.

Al told me that he had a dream in which the design of a ring

Life Is a Stamp Collection

became clear to him, and he knew that the ring was intended for me. It would have emeralds and diamonds. These were the colors of his quiet love for me.

The ring was absolutely beautiful.

We drove from Redondo Beach where we resided, to board an aircraft at LAX which would take us to the beautiful city of Guadalajara, Mexico. Since Joan and Ron Carrera had introduced Al and me, they accompanied us to Mexico.

Al and I were on our way to marrying without hopefully the airline finding out. If they did, I would be fired. I can't remember much about the flight, except that I was never so certain about anything in my life. This was finally the home of heart that I had been searching for all my life!

Metaphorically, finally, my head would rest on Al's shoulder, and together we would be a calm supportive force for, and with, each other to go through life. We agreed that we would have three children, and I agreed with myself that I wanted three boys. This would be my first and silent choice. Maybe a girl would be okay too. However, boys would be wonderful to show the world on skis, and river rafting, and hiking up a Himalayan Mountain or two, or sailing up the Amazon River and see some of the "head-hunters" that were exhibited for tourists.

We soon found that it would be difficult to get married as Al had not brought his divorce papers from his previous marriage and getting married in Mexico is not as easy as we had been led to believe. I say — Al's *previous* marriage.

When pressed, Al told me that he had indeed been married to Audrey. They had no children. Audrey was from a wealthy Los Angeles family. Her father was into sports cars, and this is where *my* Dr. Edinger first became interested in fast, flashy, expensive cars. Al would take up racing with some of the notables of the sports car racing world in California.

However, I believed Al, and now we were winging our way to the next chapter of my life. Al Edinger, M.D., and I were married, not in Guadalajara Mexico, but near it in Ajijic, Mexico.

We returned to live in the plush Rolling Hills Estates on the Palos Verdes Peninsula, a suburb of Los Angeles. Our contemporary house was a beautiful hillside home with horse property, overlooking the Los Angeles basin. At night, the lights of Los Angeles and the surrounding mountains made an exquisite backdrop for our modernistic house with glass on three sides. From then on, it was known as the "Glass House." Pictures of the home were once featured on the front as well as inside of a major magazine. We were the beautiful couple of quiet glamour: Dr. Edinger and this blond who was seventeen years his junior. Al drove dashing cars. We had wonderful friends. We attended exciting events in Beverly Hills and Palos Verdes. I was in seventh heaven.

Al was so dynamic, so handsome, so caring with his beautiful, small but expensive gifts with gently written notes. He made me feel that I was finally in a world that was equivalent to the excitement and adventures of my childhood.

Yes, this was the correct world for me.

I was now back into the realm of post-British Raj and diplomats and Taj Mahals and fine dining served by men with those elaborate headdresses in the Ambassador Hotel in the early days in New Delhi, when I was ten. This was a continuation of the world of cold-marble palaces, first-class State Department air travel, and fascinating people like Boris Lisanavitch, Edmund Hillary, Tensing Norkai, and King Tribhuvan.

When I married the love of my life, Al Edinger, I knew I could be safe in America with him forever. Since I was ten years old, I had moved every two years due to my father's Foreign Service assignments. Now, I finally felt like I was "home." I no longer had to face riding in the US State Department's four-wheel Willy's Jeeps down to the Kathmandu Bazaar for rubber, non-breathing tennis shoes and peppermint candies and rice-paper kites. I felt I was "home."

My first three months of marriage were so content, and I felt settled for the first time in my life! And we were boundlessly in love. This man, Al Edinger, MD, of Redondo Beach, California, was so caring of his patient practice. This I could see as I went with him to make house calls in one of his exciting sports cars. Yes, in those days there were house calls. And one jazzy doctor.

As I recount several of the most heart-wrenching stories of my life, I have developed an infection on my eyelid. I wanted to go to the drug store or to an ice cream shop. Anything to quelch the fever I felt all over my body, especially on the part that protects the knowing and seeing eye. I now realize my eyes had learned not to see truth of a situation, that facts could be smoothed over so as not to feel or see actual destitute life. This would not serve me well in my marriage.

Alas, after those first three exhilarating months of marriage, Al's emotional and physical love left me. I kept wondering when he would bring it up and we could get back on our wonderful safe footing. I exercised, tanned, dieted, and he continued to buy clothes and Cartier jewelry for me, so I could dress just as he wished. I felt he must know best about taste in all things for me, as he had grown up in California. And he was older.

When nothing warmed back up for us, one of his nurses tipped me off that a beautiful lady who looked like Jill St. John, named Dee Hubert, an ex-stewardess for a competitor airline, married to one of its captains, was hanging around Al in his Rivera Village/Redondo Beach medical office. The same Dee he had been seeing when Al and I first met. For at least another two years, the two of them kept lying and pretending that all was well, but that it was just me. Finally, one day I found nude pictures of Dee on our bed. Her enormous breasts were front and center. All Al's lies blew up in his face.

In retrospect, I was terribly naïve. As a youth, I had lived in Nepal and India where marriages are arranged, and young people do not date. Nor did I. In Simla, India, the beautiful Himalayan hill station of the British Raj, I had been in a "Church of England" all-girls' boarding school, Auckland House. Every morning, we knelt in Chapel before classes. For Sunday services, we walked double file to Christ Church, up the Mall from the mountainside on which Auckland House was built.

My freshman year in high school, at Woodstock Missionary School in Mussoorie, India, was my first co-ed school since grade three. I did not start dating until we returned to the States from India in 1958, when I was fifteen. In short, I was very inexperienced and innocent about life's twists and tawdry turns.

I was only a decoy in my marriage to Al. For him and Dee, ours was a marriage of convenience. That beautiful brunette had never been out of my husband's life. Not when Al and I were dating, and not when we were married.

Dee's husband, Parker, was a United Airlines pilot. They had one child, Julie. When Parker was out of town working a flight, Dee could be with Al in Redondo Beach at his physician's office, which was near those condos that *our* money had bought.

When I was out of town working a flight, Al found a way easily to be with Dee in a bedroom in our home. He took photographs of her in pornographic poses.

Al's office staff knew. They forwarded calls to him from his lady admirers.

For five years, he denied, lied, and covered up his affair with Dee. He claimed that I was jet-lagged to think such things. I was beginning to feel like the victim in the movie, *Gas Light*, in which the husband tried to make his wife feel she was losing her mind. When the evidence became unmistakable, Al ultimately admitted his infidelity. He said his relationship with Dee had remained "tumultuous and, therefore, exciting."

He said, "I truly am sorry, but Dee just would not leave me alone."

"Oh, please," I sobbed, "Just tell me once and for all, then, that I am not losing my mind, a message that you and Dee have constantly orchestrated."

I confronted Dee, "Why would you do this to your own husband and to me?"

She responded curtly, "I had wanted to ruin your relationship with Al before it could really be grounded in marriage. You took Al away from me on a level that I could not reach, by marrying him." She was deliberate.

Al was deliberate.

They willingly and intentionally messed with and hurt me, along with Captain Hubert. Their deviousness and callousness almost destroyed me.

I told Dee that I would call her husband and tell him and that I would have a letter in my safe to tell her daughter, on her sixteenth birthday.

Dee said that her husband was out working a trip, that he would be home tomorrow, and that SHE would tell him. Later, she said that he cried when she told him. How could two such immoral callous people take such liberty with the souls and devoted hearts of Captain Hubert and me?

The hardest part for me was living the lie, knowing that my marriage was in serious jeopardy, but not wanting my family to know. I was embarrassed by my naiveté.

I confided in only a very few close friends about my husband's lifestyle. When other friends and family were around, I smiled and pretended that all was well. I assumed that they did not know about my mixed-up life. Al and I continued projecting and being the beautiful couple of quiet glamour. I continued to live with Al in the Glass House. Until his next affair. Then, as calmly as possible, I told him it was his turn to move out. He owned the house with his second wife, and I had no legal right to it. But he moved.

I found out that his name was not the name that he went by or that printed on his framed medical certificates. He lied about his marriages. He lied about his age, his name, and most all other details of his life. He lied about wanting children with me. Prior to our marriage, he had given me a china and gold painted pin, of a child at a mother's breast. With this lovely, small pin, a note was written in his most beautiful handwriting. It said that he hoped I would give him a gentle child like this.

He continually lied about the most important things and details that he knew would hurt me. It was all intentional and proved that he is horridly sociopathic, and there were times I wondered if he could kill me. I had never thought the worst of people, so once again he benefitted from my lack of sophistication regarding the interaction of Americans.

Once, I was taking his jacket to the dry cleaners, and as I went through the pockets to make sure he hadn't left one of his favorite writing pens in a pocket, I brought my hand out full of slivered bones.

When I asked Al about that, he said while he was working at the emergency room of Bay Harbour Hospital in Torrance, a man was brought in. He had been bucked off a horse and hit his head on a tree stump.

I guess Al just wanted — well, I don't know why anyone would want to keep a pocket full of skull slivers.

He was still married to his second wife, Audrey, when he married me in Ajijic, Mexico. I wanted to marry someplace exotic, and he wanted to just not get caught, I suppose.

Later, Al hired a photographer to take pictures of me on a new Corvette in a blue velour jumpsuit. He unexpectedly brought the Corvette home and told me it was for me.

Some of the neighbors came out in those days and said "Doctor, what kind of car is that?" It was not a car I had asked for, and if he had asked, I would have said I would like another type of car. I already had a little red Toyota as my airport car.

Al said I should not take the plastic off the interior doors, and so I never did until he and I separated, and someone asked me about the coverings.

Inside the Iron Curtain

In early February 1970, I had an exciting adventure. I went to Budapest with a group of eight people. My husband and I were separated. It was a good time to distract me with something else. It was my first time inside an Iron Curtain country. While we were there, people celebrated Lenin's birthday. Soviet troops were everywhere, including in the hotel where we stayed.

When I encountered Soviet troops in an elevator of the hotel, they faced me and mimicked me. When the door opened at my floor and I politely said, "Excuse me, excuse me," they smiled as they said, "Coose me, coose me."

How many women have been in a closed elevator with Russian soldiers facing toward the back of the elevator all smiling and staring?

But the most exciting thing was being in a land of great musical quality, of beautifully haunting rhapsodies, and songs of mystery. (Well now, the other was exciting too.)

On my birthday, February 17, I was serenaded with the

Life Is a Stamp Collection

Hungarian version of a birthday rhapsody in a cave restaurant on the Pest side of the Danube. What a delight! It was a wonderful dinner, complete with dancers, music, and nice wines.

While in Budapest, I made friends with one of the lady tour guides, an employee of Malev Airline. It happened that she was also married to a physician, and we soon found that we had a common bond. She seemed to feel comfortable with me as she quietly told me what it was like not to have personal freedoms but added that they had "just enough" food. However, Poles were coming across the border and buying the meager meat supplies and other items of necessity while Hungarians were at work.

"One day," she said, "a group of Hungarians took off work and waited for the marauding Poles to come across the border and make their way to the Hungarian shops. Do you think they politely escorted the Poles back to the border? No. They beat them up before taking them back to their homeland!"

She told the story with a bit of humor, but underneath, she expressed a sense that they did have some personal control over their lives during the time that the Soviets kept a thumb on the collective Hungarian neck. I later told this story to Andrew Kasczak, a Polish-Canadian when he was a member of our Marco Island Philosopher's Café. He gave a reaction that I had not expected, which was one of sympathy for Polish people: "Of course, there was such lack of food and necessities during that time in Poland."

My new Hungarian friend complained that it was very difficult to get things that the ladies love—makeup, nylons, and lovely American-style clothes. They would see these things in magazines which were on the black market. With a bit of hesitation, I asked, "Would you like for me to leave with you my make-up case and maybe some nylons when I leave for New York?"

"Oh, yes," she said. Then she added quietly, "But please don't just hand them to me as you leave. Someone will be watching."

On the day of my departure, we walked over to a certain table, prearranged, in the air terminal. I leaned over and placed on the floor a brown paper bag with my nylons, shampoo, makeup and some small items of American-brand clothing. We chatted for several minutes as we observed Soviet guards with guns walking on the indoor balconies above us. Then, as we bade each other goodbye, she nonchalantly picked up the brown bag and walked away.

I have lost touch with her, and I regret that I cannot place her name in my fading memory. Our paths would never cross again. Perhaps they still will, some day. Her husband was a physician and named Phillip or Peter ... there in Budapest.

On the flight out of Budapest, I had the honor of the gods to sit with a lady who struck up a conversation about our meal. We flew to Prague before starting our long flight to New York. When we landed in Prague and taxied to the gate, Soviet soldiers boarded and stood by the front entry door. After the deplaning passengers had exited, the soldiers just stood around the cockpit and front entry door and brandished their rifles.

To get a closer glimpse of the soldiers, I walked nonchalantly into the first-class cabin. I managed this without getting shot, so my story is undoubtedly less interesting than it might have been.

After we had taken off from Prague and were at cruising altitude, my seatmate, a Hungarian Jew, told me stories of the persecution that she and her family had endured during her youth. She said that on one occasion she and others were stripped naked and made to stand in rows in a field all day long. For days, there was no water and no protection from the elements. One-by-one their heads were shaved.

She said that her husband did menial clean-up tasks, but for paid employment, he had to join the Communist party. In accented English, she continued, "This was against his principles; he did it so we could survive." She, herself, was not a communist and, therefore, was not employed.

As she continued to break my heart with her stories, she interrupted herself at one point and said, "You don't believe me, do you?"

Tears came down my cheeks as I looked at her in amazement and said, "Of course, I believe you. Why would I not?" In fact, I had only recently been reading about these same kinds of atrocities that were perpetrated against the Jews. This was in the 1970s, not that far from the time of the extreme abuse and carnage of both Jews and non-Jews in Europe. I was told that Poland had the most non-Jews executed by the Germans.

Father retired from Foreign Service

In 1972, shortly after the Indio-Pakistani war in which East Pakistan became Bangladesh, my father retired from his last tour in the Foreign Service under the Nixon administration.

Uncle Jack Craig, who was President of Union University, a Baptist University in Jackson, Tennessee, had told university officials about my father's experiences in South Asia. They asked if Daddy might be interested in teaching a course in Asian Studies. Uncle Jack called me to say he needed an answer immediately so the class could be printed in the upcoming schedule of courses.

But, due to the eight day war, with Pakistan, Daddy and my mother were trapped inside India. I decided to go as far as I could get toward India and then, somehow, get inside the country to bring my parents' home. I called Pan Am and asked, "May I have your schedule for Flight #1 to New Delhi? Would it be better if I went via the Pacific or the Atlantic route, since I will be on standby?"

"What do you mean you want to go to Delhi? No aircraft are going into or out of that airport. Only military jets are using it!"

I was concerned but had no intense fear for myself. After all, when I was there as a child, there had been student riots in Nepal outside the American Library, and at times, we were confined inside our palace compound. So, I didn't think a war should be that big of a deal. I now realize that I must have sounded like I had been smoking a hookah or something. I simply wanted to get my parents out of India, but I could not go.

As they prepared to leave India, Mother said she had to pack by flashlight as there was a blackout over New Delhi.

A night-watchman outside their flat gave a shrill whistle of reprimand when he saw their light shining behind the curtains.

Anyway, we got a call from New York that my parents had been flown safely out. They received the message about the position at the University of Tennessee, Martin Branch, and yes, Daddy was interested in the teaching position for Asian Studies. The gods had given my parents a direction in which to go with their lives and at a good location near the Kentucky border in Tennessee.

On my days off from flying, to get a respite from my troubled marriage, I began frequently to visit my little oceanfront lot in Punta Bandera, Mexico, on the upper coastline of the Pacific that Al and I had purchased to build our dream home. The drive from Los Angeles to Tijuana would take me past the flower-growing fields in Carlsbad. I would view the rows and rows and more rows of multi-colored blooms of flowers which were being grown simply for seed. These seeds would be shipped all over the world. The flowers were the same color as the precious stones that I remembered seeing in the Taj Mahal, in Agra, before they were dug out by thieves.

Japanese-Americans kept up our yards, and Mexicans worked in our homes. As I travelled so much, I was always grateful that I had help to keep up my house.

Sometimes, government helicopters would swoop down over the workers in the flower fields. The illegal aliens would scatter like a frightened herd to their hiding places in the earth beside the access road, La Costa Blvd. The local California owner was never reprimanded, as Mexican labor was being used as common laborers and domestics everywhere.

It was only about thirty more miles to the border with Mexico. And, yes, there was a fence with holes and patches in it. Mexican youth sat on the knoll just above the Tijuana River and taunted the US Border Control agents.

I passed by La Jolla in a blur as, by then, I was anxious to get to the Hotel Del Coronado on lovely, sunny Coronado Island. There I would have lunch and a quick look into the hotel shops. It is a fabulous hotel, with the great history of President Nixon hosting Mexico's President Diaz Ordaz there. Also, after Prince of Wales abdicated, he visited the hotel, which now sports the Prince of Wales Grill!

After lunch, I proceeded through Chula Vista and San Ysidro on the US side and crossed into Mexico. There I found myself in the very uncolorful environment of potholes in the pavement and shacks made of flimsy cardboard and tin in which enormous throngs of humanity lived, only a stone's throw from the most fortunate country on earth.

I navigated along the US borderline fence and dodged emaciated dogs, belonging to no one, wandering about aimlessly.

The atmosphere was one of freedom for me. To this foreigner, the positives far outweighed the negatives. The Mexican people always wanted to please. They were genuine. They had the gift of survival, even though the laws of their country and the Catholic church kept them suppressed.

The people had always been accommodating to my husband and me. Now, just to me.

The Watergate Trial

Carmen Fowler, a delightfully practical and beautiful flight attendant who was a few years younger, and I were domiciled at different West Coast bases. But somehow, we ended up working the same flight from Los Angeles to Dulles (IAD). We arrived in Washington during the Watergate Trial, which took place for about a year beginning in May 1972. At Carmen's suggestion, we sat in on the trial for a few hours during our twenty-four-hour layover. I was astounded that a layperson could go into what I assumed were the most august of proceedings.

We rose early for the occasion. A group of hippies met us as we approached the courthouse. Apparently, they had taken it upon themselves to administer control over regular people like us who wanted to observe history being made in Judge Sirica's courtroom. They gave each of us a number for entry into the court room as a seat became vacated.

We stood in a drizzly rain, waiting. At 8:00 a.m., the doors were unlocked. The hippies allowed us to get in out of the misting rain and stand in a row against the marble wall leading to the courtroom and wait. As we waited, John Mitchell and Bob Haldeman passed by. Carmen called out, "Good morning, Mr. Mitchell. Good morning, Mr. Haldeman."

Mr. Haldeman did not respond, but Mitchell gruffed out, "Good morning." Wow! He spoke to us!

As seats became vacated in the courtroom, a bailiff let some of us enter, according to the hippies' organized line. Finally, there was a seat for me, a chair right next to Mrs. Bob Haldeman. Fantastic! I was right in a front row with an unobstructed view.

Herb W. Kalmbach, Nixon's attorney, was being questioned by the prosecutor, Archibald Cox. Once in a while, the prosecutor would turn his back to the court, bring out a piece of beef jerky from his pocket, and quickly take a chew. I presume that he did this to retain a blood sugar level; the proceedings were undoubtedly draining.

During much of the time we were there, Judge Sirica had his head bent down. I wondered if he was having a quick little catnap. Was he bored? Was he reading a novel while all this was going on?

John Mitchell and Bob Haldeman were sitting to the right of Mrs. Haldeman and me. I could easily view their expressions. There were no smiles. At one point, when a question was asked regarding the behavior of Bob Haldeman, I somehow made an inaudible, but apparently noticeable, wince. Mrs. Haldeman focused a pointed, dirty look at me, so I certainly didn't do that a second time. I also noticed that as Mr. Mitchell sat with his face resting on his fist and arm, that they were very flesh tone, in contrast to his face, which was beet red.

While the prosecutor, Archibald Cox was questioning Herb Kalmbach, Nixon's personal attorney, the latter broke down. He lost control of his voice and emotions. I felt sorry for him. Apparently, Judge Sirica did, too. He asked Herb—by now, I felt that we were on a first-name basis—if he would like to take a break.

Life Is a Stamp Collection

The answer was a gentle, "Yes, your Honor."

As Carmen and I absented ourselves to leave the courtroom I thought, *how lucky can I be, to have observed some of this remarkable history in the making.*

Chapter Eight

Farrokh of Iran

It was a beautiful flight. The sun's rays bounced off the wings into the interior of the First-Class cabin. The aircraft slowly changed position. We were now heading in a more westerly route toward the Pacific Ocean. Yea! LA!

I was separated from Al and feeling free and mentally good. I was free from my eight years of "gaslight" experiences with Al Edinger, and I was bound now for home and new adventures where I would be more in control of my own life.

As the captain followed instructions from ground control to change settings, I felt a slight shift of the aircraft in my knees. I walked up the aisle on the left side of the 747, loitering a bit, so that if someone wanted something they could call out the familiar, "Oh, Miss!" and I could turn, smile, and hope the request would be for something that was actually in the limited stores of the aircraft. We had just finished serving lunch to these New Yorkers and Los Angelinos. Some PG version of a prescreened Hollywood film was on the screen. Everyone was quiet, sleeping, or enjoying the movie as I returned aft to the rear of the three-quarter screen which gave privacy for the piano bar behind the last row of coach. The piano bar was an actual piano! On top of the bar were pretzels, a beer keg, and peanuts in medium-sized baskets. Frankie Sinatra, Jr., had been booked on a 747 flight to play for the introduction of this new attraction on American Airline's trips into JFK.

I could stand, looking forward over the top of the bulkhead screen, and observe the cabin. I could see if anyone needed anything. We could know without being right in their faces.

So, as my friend Sharon, another flight attendant, and I mischievously lowered our faces and let just our eyes be visible over the bulkhead screen looking forward, the most handsome Middle Eastern man walked down the aisle toward us. There we were, with a row of eyes peeking up and over into the cabin.

Oh, my goodness, he looked just like the Shah of Iran! I quickly straightened up and pretended to be the age that I was, which was thirty-three. And of course, it was my responsibility to ask this dark, handsome man with a fantastic smile, before Sharon did, if he needed anything.

He said, "Hi. I'm Farrokh Hirbod. I am going to Los Angeles to see my children, who are half American, in Beverly Hills. I had a marriage to an American woman some years ago, although I now live in Tehran."

I said, "You look very much like the Shah."

"Well, the Queen thinks so too. She and I, along with her team, worked on a school project in one of the outlying areas of Iran. When I was first introduced to her, she did a bit of a double take."

I could see why.

Later, near the end of the flight, Farrokh asked rather shyly if I would have dinner with him in Beverly Hills the following evening.

"Yes, I would be delighted."

At that dinner, a whirlwind romance began. With an expression that was rather funny coming from an Iranian, he explained his shotgun marriage to an American woman whom he met while studying architecture in LA some years back. His desire now was to retire from and sell his architectural firm in Tehran and start bringing his money out of Iran. He said repeatedly, "The Shah will fall. Yes, the Shah will fall."

Over the next several months, Farrokh and I saw each other often. He commuted back and forth from Tehran to Los

Angeles. I continued to work my flight assignments and, quite often, would meet him in New York. Even though Farrokh would be exhausted from his international flights, he was the perfect companion, a real gentleman. Being with him was like being in a fairytale. We were a most distinguished couple, with his handsome looks, tan skin, and graying hair and my blonde hair and blue eyes.

On one occasion when we were in Manhattan, he told me that he needed to deposit some of the money that he would be bringing out of Iran from the sale of his architectural firm. We went to a well-known American-based New York bank the next morning. Indeed, he did open an account and deposited a large sum of money. As we exited, the manager of the bank, with a wide smile, very smartly held the door open for us. I am sure he was thinking that there would be more to come. There was.

Then, Farrokh told me that he had put a deposit on a high-rise condominium. He wanted me to see it. By taxi, he took me to Olympic Towers, a tall condominium building that Aristotle Onassis was having built in New York. As we got out of the taxi, I looked up and marveled at the height of this fabulous structure. Olympic Towers. It looked like it could just about reach an American Airlines jet taking off from LaGuardia Airport!

It had not been so many years ago, September 1963, that I had asked for a base assignment in New York. Upon my graduating from stewardess flight school, that is precisely what happened. New York was then the culmination of glamour. It was the era and the atmosphere of *Breakfast at Tiffany's* when I moved to 65th and York on the Upper East Side.

So, that was then.

This was now. 1975. I knew that I had been led down this road for Farrokh and me to meet, and these were the events that I was to experience next in my life. This handsome Iranian, Farrokh Hirbod, was to be my life's partner. My life was finally coming together.

The building was only partially completed, but Farrokh and I were given yellow hard hats and escorted inside. The construction was taking place just across from St. Patrick's

Cathedral. We ascended to the floor where the model condominium was located, which Farrokh wanted me to see. I could not quite get my mind around how these wonderful events were unfolding so quickly. It was almost too much. We had known each other only a short time.

So, on this day we were looking at the model that Farrokh wanted me to see. He had previously put a down payment on a specific condo. "Do you like it?"

"Of course, I do. Your taste is fabulous!"

He said, "Now I want to show you Onassis's own condo. They say he is willing to sell it."

We viewed what we were told had been the choice apartment of Ari Onassis, the one he had held in reserve for himself. It was several open floors with a very narrow, straight-down view of St. Patrick's Cathedral, out the south multi-storied window. There were to be shear curtains.

Our dating took place mostly in New York while I was on layovers with my work trips. We were always in a beautiful restaurant, eating, listening to jazz, talking with heads together, infatuated, so much in love.

As the weeks went by, Farrokh and I looked at many small business properties near the Palos Verdes Peninsula in California. At his request, I purchased several of them in my name. He would pay for them with checks drawn on his account in the New York bank.

One day Farrokh said, "I want us to look for a house. You choose where you want it, and we will get a real estate agent and see as many houses as it takes for you to find the perfect one. I just want you to be happy, and if you are happy, I will be too. I know you don't want to continue to live in your Glass House, so we will have the condo in New York and a home in California, and then we will make a decision about a place in Europe."

"Will there not be a home for us in Tehran?" I asked disappointedly.

"No. The shah will fall."

That was the only thing Farrokh would deny me.

One time Farrokh arrived from Tehran with a lovely gift for me. It was a beautiful large, egg-sized emerald surrounded with smaller diamonds. The chain and the mounting which held it was also encrusted with diamonds. He presented it to me in a soft bag. By now, I was not surprised by the beautiful gifts that this handsome man constantly presented me. To get it through US Customs, Farrokh had put the jewel in a Band-Aid tin. He was learning that New York customs always harassed him a bit, asking where his prayer rug was in his luggage.

Farrokh seemed to take everything in stride. He had been raised in Iran, where his father was the Minister of Fisheries. Farrokh had studied in Switzerland and at the University of Southern California.

While Farrokh was in Tehran, the real estate agent and I looked for the perfect home on the Southern California Palos Verdes Peninsula. I could think of no place more beautiful. This would be our primary residence. One day my agent called and said, "Angela, I have found a lovely Mediterranean home overlooking San Pedro and the Long Beach Harbor. It will not last."

That evening around 6:00 p.m., she took me to see the home. It was absolutely beautiful. It would be a peaceful home in which to raise those three boys I had always planned to have. The view was wonderful, with the twilight of twinkling lights unfolding below in a magic carpet.

But Farrokh was in Tehran. He wouldn't be able to see it before I had to make a decision. An authentic-looking Mediterranean home with exquisite cypress trees flanking the front yard would not last. This I knew. I asked the agent to offer a price which seemed ridiculous, a price that just popped into my head. I have a good intuition about property, and I wish it could be said the same about men.

The owners accepted, although they were skeptical about the contingency that the money would be delivered by hand from Tehran in two weeks, when the amount would be paid in full.

When Farrokh saw the house, he was as captivated as I was.

We set about purchasing the perfect furniture and beautiful carpets for this home on Altimira Street in Rolling

Hills. Some of the furniture from my Glass House also went into it. To this day, I have a mint-green, grand Kerman rug under my dining room table. In the carpet store, this 9' x 14' carpet was suspended on a wall with lights shining on it. When I suddenly turned and saw it, it was breathtaking. I knew that Farrokh would indulge me.

When we purchased new items for the house, Farrokh would often bargain with the manager for a better price. Even in Bullock's Department Store! I had never seen this done in America, though the process was familiar to me. In Asia, one always had to bargain. It was the way of business on the street, and it was the way of corporate business in America. Yes, I knew I was now back in my proper stride. This was the familiar. This was the way I had been raised in Asia.

We proceeded to buy more things for the house. We traveled to Belgium for tapestries, France for antiques, and Switzerland just for some good chocolates. We had a 450 SEL Mercedes Benz automobile custom made. It was silver with a navy-blue interior. Farrokh indulged me it was a car that I absolutely loved. We picked up the car in Stuttgart, Germany, and drove it around Europe. My conservative, *when I wanted to be*, European blood seemed to think that putting miles on it would make the duty less at US Customs in LAX.

Finally, our days of touring were finished, and we delivered the car to a Lufthansa Airlines freight location in Frankfurt Airport. The car was flown FRA to LAX with my airline discount. This makes me chuckle that I used a discount to fly a 450 SEL Mercedes home. Farrokh could not have cared less.

There was never a time that I observed Farrokh being anything but ethical. He was talented, wealthy, generous, and, well, always around. I was his world, as he didn't need to work. I was not used to this kind of attention. It was very flattering after the marriage that I'd had with Al Edinger.

When I came in from working flights, Farrokh was there. When I shopped, he was there. He encouraged me to buy everything I liked for our house, and I did.

The Golden Cage

With no free time, I was beginning to feel a bit stressed. I had far too little attention from Al when I was married and loved and lived with him. Now I was Farrokh's complete world.

He had visits with his children, who lived in the San Fernando Valley, and now he had fewer visits to Tehran.

I was still working flights. I felt that perhaps this would not be the time to quit my job as a stewardess. Not just yet. When I was gone from Farrokh, I was with passengers and crew constantly, and when I returned from a trip, I was with him nonstop until my next scheduled flight. I encouraged him to start painting with all the supplies he had bought when he first told me of his passion for art and his desire to resume painting. He now had the time as his firm had been sold and all monies were transferred to the bank in New York.

One day we traveled to downtown Los Angeles to the office of a famous attorney in a beautiful skyscraper to have a prenuptial agreement drawn up. The agreement was very generous in my favor.

I introduced Farrokh to all the couple-friends that Al and I had when we were married. I felt that he needed some men in his life for balance.

Farrokh and Tom, a doctor who had a great escapist imagination, became friends. They talked about writing and presenting papers to the United Nations on solutions for world peace. Inventions that were entirely unrealistic would be spelled out, and excitement would sweep Farrokh outside of conventional reality.

When we traveled, Farrokh worried about the least little health situation. If someone had a cold in the same room, he would immediately start using medicine. My reality check for my life was starting to give me a sinking feeling in my stomach.

What was I to do? I couldn't have another human being feel the way I had when I was married to Al. I needed to give this relationship my best try, and one more time, I began to sublimate myself to please someone. I did not want to hurt

Farrokh. He had been so generous with me, with his heart, with the many gifts, and with the fun we had shared.

Farrokh trusted me. He purchased properties all over the Los Angeles area and put them in my name. He was not a US citizen then, and he said this made things easier.

We cruised on a river off Morea, Fiji, where we bought many works of art from the indigenous tribes to be framed in Los Angeles. We said that we would never ever forget how we felt for each other. Ever.

But deep down, I wanted to be financially independent. Therefore, I continued to work so I could be independent from Farrokh in that regard. I kept my schedule of flight assignments and, along with Farrokh, oversaw the remodeling and redecorating of our beautiful new Mediterranean-style home.

I also monitored the house that I had shared with Al, the Glass House. This would be granted to me with the divorce when that time arrived.

Farrokh and I traveled from Europe to the South Pacific and purchased beautiful items. At the same time, the walls were closing in, and I was starting to need more space emotionally, and as with all airline people, my job meant that I was continuously with others, meeting their needs. I was with others constantly, and I was with this wonderful man constantly.

When I left for work, Farrokh was there. When I returned from work, Farrokh was there to greet me and to say that he wanted to go out to dinner and go dancing after a romantic dinner. He was always so glad to see me when I returned. He had no other interests, so I mustered up the energy to be a good companion. For my part, I was tired. For hours, I had walked across the nation in a tube going 500 miles an hour.

I listened to his stories of inventions. They were of many things of which I could not comprehend. All seemed so futuristic. Then I listened to more of his thoughts on inventions, and then more, and then more. His thinking seemed innocent and hopeful.

Mine was too realistic for my years.

I did not want to see that there might possibly be a road of no eventual reasonable intertwining of our two cultures.

Culture? And to what culture did I belong? I had lived in three countries, and my family had lived in four.

Books have been written about children, called "Third Culture Kids," who were raised outside their home countries. These are children born of parents of one nationality, but who are raised in several other countries. When these TCKs are brought back to their birth country as adults, they are never quite sure that this is where they belong. However, whenever they travel, or are confronted with a new situation, they usually are the most adaptable, comfortable citizens of the world. My heart's beacon was always America.

Farrokh and I continued with our individual logic, borne of our different backgrounds. I chose to keep my job, as once again it was the rock into which I could keep my toes curled. The job would always be there. It kept me on a predestined course, it seemed. No matter how much I wanted to leave my job of being a flight attendant, it was always safely there to cushion me when my dreams evaporated.

But now I had to work very hard to emotionally maintain this relationship. Farrokh's every waking wish was to please me. I was his sole world.

Then, it seemed that the Middle Eastern dominant religion of Islam with Allah was becoming his sole world, as I quietly receded. Everything would be so perfect if I could only not mind constant companionship, constant attention, and constant scrutiny. I could not mesh my earlier feelings with his expectations for us.

Soon the inquisitions started. When I entered a room after having a phone conversation in another nearby room, he would ask, "Why are you pale? Was that a man on the phone with whom you were talking?"

I was stunned. With all the education in non-Middle Eastern countries this man had, I would never have thought that he would have reverted to the ways of a sixth-century tribe! Control and manipulation of a woman. Perhaps he had seen this with the female members of his family in Iran. Of course, he had.

I asked myself if I could learn to live with this attitude. We went to Dr. Johnson in Beverly Hills and tried counseling together, but I knew in my heart of hearts that I could not again deny who I was. I could not go through yet another relationship in which my every thought and move were scrutinized. But, how to start undoing all the promises I had made?

I tried to make the relationship somehow jump-start again. Over and over, I talked to myself about seeing the material aspect of things and about what all would have to be undone, and why couldn't I just live with the thought that I would never have to worry about money again.

Slowly but surely the golden cage started fastening around me, tighter and tighter. Gifts became lovelier along with promises to change, and all reasons for my claustrophobia inside the "golden world" would be lifted.

Alas, I could go not one more inch inside that world.

In front of lawyers, I began signing quitclaim deeds to the many valuable properties that were in my name, reverting them to Farrokh. There were business properties along major boulevards in Beverly Hills, in several LA towns, and elsewhere. There were bank accounts. I closed our mutual bank accounts and turned all monies over to him. I wanted nothing from this man who didn't understand why I couldn't live in his world of control. I felt horrible for his sake that I could not, and I felt such disappointment for my sake.

I moved back to the Glass House, taking the furniture that I had moved from it. I kept a Cluny copy Belgium tapestry, the mint-green Iranian grand Kerman rug, and a corner inlaid mother-of-pearl piece of furniture with Arabic Koran script. I left Farrokh everything else.

I started to be able to take a deep breath without someone looking over my shoulder asking why was I sighing: Was I thinking of a lover? Was I seeing someone else?

I couldn't get on an airplane fast enough to work my assigned trips.

Farrokh left for Tehran, where he could try to grapple with this situation and be with his close friends. As I returned our joint California land purchases to Farrokh by quitclaim deed, I felt no regret because fairy tales do sometimes come true, but I didn't think that this would be the case for us. There really did not seem to be an anchor for holding aloft this beautiful magic carpet we were on.

Farrokh told the lawyer that he wanted me to have the Mercedes Benz sedan we had built in Germany, as it was my wish and he bought it for me. I accepted the car.

Dissolved Marriage

It was late 1975. I had not counted on being in a dissolved marriage, as it would be described in California in those days AND a dissolved relationship with Farrokh. Never, ever.

I felt numb as Al and I stood before the judge, who said, "You, Angela Edinger, are gainfully employed by American Airlines. There are no children. Therefore, there will be no spousal support."

I wanted to say to the judge, "Thank heavens for my job; it has sustained me, given my life a focus away from the gaslight environment into which I married." Of course, I didn't.

The judge continued: "You accepted division of material property, and it is as you have settled. Angela Edinger, two cars, the home in Rolling Hills Estates on the Palos Verdes Peninsula (the Glass House), and the property in Baja, Mexico are yours. Dr. Edinger, the additional properties in California are yours." Down went the gavel.

The sound resounded in my ears, not a literal gavel, but the sound of my heart imploding in a crushing spiral. The beautiful brunette had outdone the naïve blonde.

The Baja lot in Mexico and the Glass House were left to me in the divorce! Al must have thought that with two marriages biting the dust in it, he would just put it on my side of the divorce settlement ledger. Well, that was fine with me, because now the cat and I would not have to move as we had previously with each altercation.

After our divorce, Al went into the Air Force since Congress was asking for professionals, such as lawyers and MDs, to come back into the military. They gave them a higher rank as it was hard to keep professional men enlisted.

I was alone. Each day, I would put one foot in front of the other, leave the house, get into my car, and leave behind my anchoring. My harbor. My Glass House. I would maneuver carefully onto Los Angeles 405 Freeway. Then I would look down to see what I was wearing. If I was in uniform, then I must be going to work, and I would continue toward LAX. If I was in a regular dress, then I must be going to Beverly Hills to Dr. Johnson's office. Dr. Johnson, a southern gentleman, had been referred to me by a Chinese friend, Audrey. He was the perfect person to talk with, to be counseled by. He had come from Kentucky and could perhaps understand my background better than most people in Beverly Hills. I would rest my stunned psyche on an imaginary shoulder.

The time came when these consultations, which had been reasonably effective, were no longer needed for me to regain my balance. I had been less than forthcoming to my parents about these therapy sessions, but once I told them, my father said, "Well, now you have had enough." Stalwart people, as he had taught us to be, were not to be weak, would not divorce, and certainly would not need a psychiatrist.

Divorce had never happened in our family. I was the oldest child and the oldest grandchild. Divorce, after only eight years of marriage, was certainly no fine example for others! I was breaking new, negative ground for my family, and it embarrassed my mother terribly. Perhaps my father too. But it was she, not he, who said, "Honey, are you cheating on Al?"

Later, I would joke to my friends that my husband got the condos on the beach in Redondo Beach, California, and I got this little lemon piece of property in Mexico.

However, it soon dawned on me that I would need to come up with much more cash to keep funding this Mexican ranchero home. As I asked the Divine how to manage this, it came to me that I should put the Glass House in Rolling Hills up for sale and get out from under its bad karma. I thought I might move over closer to Malibu and Brentwood.

As things unfolded and no property interested me in those suburbs, a light bulb went off in my head, and the thought that I should move to Mexico became more and more definite for me. I would move there and then later purchase another California home within the time limits to avoid capital gains taxes.

The Right Reverend Monsignor

The brothers, Pedro and Raul Lopez Gallo, whom I had met when Al and I purchased the Mexican property before our divorce, were pressuring me to build on the property soon. In Mexico, one paid in cash as they built as there were no bank loans. Pedro and Raul said they would help me. If I would give them my Mercedes SEL as a down payment for the construction, they would give me credit for it.

Okay, that worked for me! I bought into this hook, line, and sinker. The Mercedes became the down payment for the structure Al and I had previously planned to build together. Pedro Lopez Gallo agreed to start building a house on this exquisite lot above the Pacific Ocean, in Baja Calif, Mexico.

Pedro owned the lots in Punta Bandera just below Tijuana. Foreigners cannot own land near the Pacific Ocean but must lease it for thirty years. That was the only option then, and still may be.

Pedro was a very nice man. After we became better acquainted, I dated him a few times with a brief romantic encounter or two. He told me that one time he had gone on an overland camel caravan from Baghdad to Tehran. I was so naïve. In my typical blonde fashion, I said, "Where did you go to the bathroom?"

He shouted, "BATHROOM! WHAT BATHROOM?"

He said when they arrived in Tehran, he stayed in the shower almost a whole day trying to get clean from all the grit in parts of the body he didn't even know he had.

His story made me chuckle.

In Baja, while helping me build the house, Pedro introduced me as his fiancée. I went along with it to others, and pretending was not so hard as he was inordinately handsome. I

I will always be grateful for the beautiful pink casa my Catholic priest and I built. This was in 1977.

I asked Raul and his beautiful wife, Mary, if Pedro was married, which I had just assumed he was not. Raul answered, "Not exactly."

One day an American told me my landlord and sometimes date was *Father* Pedro Lopez Gallo, the Right Reverend Monsignor Pedro Lopez Gallo. My *friend* Pedro had neglected to tell me he was a priest in the Vatican in Rome. When I confronted him, he said, "Well, Angelita, in a man's lifetime is he not many things?"

I said, "Well, Pedro, this is quite serious as I don't think God is amused about the Roman Catholic sect dating women."

Pedro had business in Rome and Mexico City, and he seemed to be out of the country quite often. Occasionally I would hear that he was in Rome, and his brother Raul was not quite sure when he would be back.

Later, when Pedro came back from Rome, he took me to his condo on the other side of the border in San Diego, and I saw a lovely teenage girl in a photo frame sitting on the bar. I also saw a picture of Pedro with his mother and Pope John Paul.

I asked who the young girl was, and he explained that she was the daughter of his mistress in the south of France. Daughter of his what? In the south of France? Wow!

Pedro responded, "Well, Angelita, she says this is my child, but how is one to know?" *Angelita didn't really know either, you see.*

Pedro and Father Ratzinger (Pope Benedict) were roommates at one time. They were in a photograph in *Time* magazine, talking together in their magenta-colored priestly ensembles! Pedro really was a PRIEST. Ahh!

Once in Tijuana, drugs were planted in Mary's (his niece's) husband's car, and he was arrested at the US border. It was at the border crossing of San Ysidro, which I had passed through for many years, as did thousands of Mexicans and some Americans daily.

A few years later, I saw on the Internet, the letters Pedro wrote on Vatican letterhead stationery to the San Diego courts, telling them of what a good and honorable man Mary's husband was.

Back in the late 1970s when I lived full time below Tijuana, in Punta Bandera, sometimes I was asked by Pedro's brother, Raul, to take Raul's children, little Mary and Raulita, across the border to their American grade school. I did.

After I had lived in Florida for a time, I looked up Pedro and sent him an e-mail.

He was head of a Catholic boy's school in Vancouver, Canada. He called, and we talked. I asked him if his life had turned out the way he wanted. Since he was the youngest of seven brothers, I believe, he was the one designated to be the priest.

He said, "Well, mostly."

Pedro called me in the mid-2000s, leaving messages on my cell phone, which I left on the phone so I could listen to them again at my whim.

Around his eightieth birthday, he told me that a few Cardinals would be travelling to Guadalajara with him to celebrate his birthday, as that was where it all started.

Chapter Nine

Peru

My friend Dana and I decided we should go to Peru, to Machu Picchu, and up the Amazon, you know, well, as long as it is there ….

We boarded Avianca Airlines out of LAX, and as we were walking down the aisle into our area, we heard someone call our names! Two AA flight attendants we knew were sitting further back, and we discovered that they were going on this same tour.

After arriving in Lima and transferring to our hotel, we had a lovely dinner of Peruvian national food while discussing sightseeing events for the next day. There were many interesting historical museums, of course, and a gold museum which was just spectacular.

After some local sightseeing and visiting their museums, we were ready to leave by flight to Cusco.

We arrived in Cusco, and it was cold at an elevation of approximately 13,000 feet. That night I slept in double layers of clothing. The scenery of the Andes was breathtaking as we went on drives to various nearby locations. Lake Titicaca, with stones stacked on top of each other around the lake, was one of them. We went up to Pisac at approximately 14,000 ft, to *Sabado Mercado*, the Saturday market.

There I bought watercolor paintings; though they were small, the intimate life of Peruvian culture showed through.

Then another day, we four boarded a train to go down to Machu Picchu. Its elevation is at approximately 8,000 feet.

A Mormon businessman, Hiram Bingham, had flown over the bit of jungle which covered over possibly the lost city of the Incas. Or so they thought. I read that Hiram B. hiked down and discovered the location of a former city. He was photographing for *National Geographic*. Supposedly the place was terribly overgrown and crawling with thousands of snakes. They brought in black pigs to rout them out and eat them.

So, of course by the time we four arrived, there were hundreds of stone steps up to almost every level. All overgrowth had been cleared!

Much later, someone commented that I was leaning at a right angle, up against a group of rock formations in all their photos! Well, yes, the air is thinner at such altitudes, and I felt I could breathe better while leaning over. One must, I say, "breathe."

While in Cusco, a parade came down the street in the waning sun of the evening. A statue of the Virgin Mary stood in the back of a truck as musicians played crude horns, making as much music as they could.

The Indians stopped to watch, as we did, though we were neither locals, Indians, nor in my case, Catholic. I am not sure if I had decided if I were Buddhist or not at this point.

The sculptor, his family and me

Life Is a Stamp Collection

We were told about an indigenous man, poor and common, who had taken the top honor for sculpture in Peru.

We were asked if we would like to meet him as he lived in Cusco.

"Oh, yes, absolutely," was our reply.

Soon we were in the front of his small home which he shared with his wife and four or five children.

I asked if I could purchase some of his work, something small which could fit in my suitcase. Indeed, he had a portrait of an old Peruvian Indian with a crown of thorns, hanging on a bark cross. I managed to get it home to California where I simply placed it on a closet shelf.

The Cross

In one of our many earthquakes in southern California, the whole house shook for quite a few seconds. Minutes. The

Peruvian cross rolled off its holding shelf and onto the carpeted floor. The beige, clay Christ broke right off of his bark cross.

I simply picked it up and placed the pieces into a box, thinking I would not throw this wonderful memento away, but just hold it safely until I thought of what to do with it.

Several years later, I moved to another state.

After 9-11, when I moved out of my condo and into my house, my brother Roger, was visiting. I showed him the Peruvian Christ and explained how it had lived through one of my California earthquakes, but not perfectly.

He wired it together, so that once again the parts were in the correct place, but now, it was a little more crude. And a bit more authentic!

So, back to Cusco, Peru, where the four of us flew out to Lima and connected to Iquitos, Peru.

Here we boarded a claptrap open airboat for sailing up a tributary of the Amazon. It just so happened that half of a floorboard was missing. As I stepped onto this luxury liner, I sprained my ankle. Luckily, I had elastic bandages in my suitcase for such occurrences.

Mexico

It was time to do something about the land in Mexico. I got busy getting names in Baja to help me with my move. Pedro got my electricity turned on and other helpful issues, like installing a propane tank at the side of my house. I had purchased a gas stove at Montgomery Ward that did not need an electronic ignition.

One day, I looked up, and there was a turquoise flatbed truck with my household goods on it, waiting to be moved into my house. At that time, there were torrential rains there in upper Baja. Roads were washed out, and officials from Mexico City were there. It was harder to get things delivered without the *mordida*, which means "the bite" or bribe.

My dog, Sasha

My dog, Sacha, and I moved in. The waves were awesome and, with the wind howling, I put a few logs into the fireplace, and we became toasty warm again. My blue suede sofa did not get *too* wet, but it would dry, I told myself.

View of the Pacific

A few days later, the giant Pacific Ocean swells calmed. As the sun came out, I could see across the ten miles to the four islands known as the "Three Sisters," as visually, only three islands could be seen. I had never seen such beauty on the water! It was like being in an altered universe.

The electricity was iffy, the water pipes were breaking under my Mexican designed tile, and I did not know about water regulators for new construction.

My house was painted pale pink and had the typical red-tiled roof. It was just perfect, except for now needing an electrical regulator for the refrigerator. No one told me. Would I ever not cry myself to sleep, again? Yes, the wrought iron gates to my tiled open patio were so very Spanish, and just beautiful, if I do say so myself. The two windows of stained glass in the shape of a bull's eye looked attractive at night with a light behind each.

Quite often, when I was returning from San Diego airport crossing the border into Mexico, I drove past the new bull ring. As I proceeded onward towards Punta Bandera, I saw spouts of air/mist coming from the whales' blowholes being caught in the air and sunshine.

Each year, the whale pods began their migration from their feeding grounds down to the lower Mexican Baja peninsula, where they gave birth. Their birthing bays are Laguna San Ignacio, Laguna Ojo de Liebre, San Ignacio Lagoon, and Magdalena. The grey whale lives in the eastern Pacific Alaskan waters in the summer. What they eat must be stored up for their trip south. If they do eat while heading south, the whale goes to the ocean floor, rolls onto its side, and eats small fish. They travel approximately seventy-five miles a day at a speed of five miles an hour.

I saw the whales migrating south to bear their young in one of their many birthing bays in lower Baja. On the return trip from the birthing lagoon, whales stay closer to the shore as they proceeded northward. What a glorious sight! I sensed their freedom and happiness of having added to their pod family. A mother with a new baby whale and an auntie would travel together, as the auntie could keep the baby buoyant while it suckled.

Punta Bandera and Donald Trump

My friend, Reiko Tachibano, from Narita, Japan, who had helped me with interpretation while I was in the Red Cross hospital in 2000, came to visit me in Florida around 2006. We traveled from Florida to San Diego, rented a car, and drove to Punta Bandera. As I was turning into this beautiful area of Punta Bandera, Donald Trump's face was on a huge billboard at the top of the cobblestone road, advertising very tall buildings with individual condos here in Baja, Mexico! Wow!

I was so impressed that the man from *The Apprentice* saw such value in my beautiful, oceanfront, zen-energy area right next door! The lot was empty of buildings, but one small cement house stood there. Huge holes had been dug with yellow International Harvester equipment which now idled on the lot. It looked as if a project was starting to be materialized but suddenly stopped!

After I returned to Florida, I looked up on the internet

about the progress on this Trump property. There had been some misunderstanding between Donald Trump and his investors, as it was stated that he said that he had only licensed his name. Many Californians had invested in it, and Ivanka Trump was now handling it, saying to the people that they knew they could always trust in the Trump name.

The next time I saw the Trump family was in real life at the University of Pennsylvania Wharton School of Business graduation for my niece, Alexis Sanders. Alexis procured seats under a covering in the bleachers. I looked down, and the Trump family was moving into one row, with Eric, Donald Jr, The Donald, and Melania. From the other side, Ivana and an older woman, perhaps her mother, entered and sat next to Eric. From the back, someone called out, "Hey, Donald!" Donald turned facing all us and waved. Very nice of him.

Then graduation started, and names were called out as the students lined up. When my niece, Alexis Sanders was called, it was stated that she had the distinction of graduating as a "Joseph Wharton Scholar!" Later my sister Brenda and I treated all for a nice Philadelphia luncheon.

Chapter Ten

Michener/ Caravans/Afghanistan

How did Michener really manage to capture all this into one book? *Caravans*.

Once when I was spending a lot of time in and out of Los Angeles, I saw a TV program about the LA Explorers Club. Sir Edmund Hillary had recently spoken there. I called the Club and said I would like to join. There was dead silence on the other end. Then, laughter. The man on the other end told me, almost incredulously, "It's for men ONLY, No women allowed—only men." Hadn't they heard about Gloria Steinem?

Thirty years later, when I showed them my photo of Sir Edmund Hillary signing my autograph book, I was allowed to join the *National* Chapter of the Explorers Club of Naples, Florida.

While I continued to live and work flights in and out of Los Angeles, my mother recommended that I read Michener's *Caravans*. She and my father had traveled to Kabul for a vacation while they were posted in New Delhi, about 1970, where Father was part of the American technical assistance team. Mother said, "If I had read *Caravans* before we went, I don't think I would have gone to Afghanistan." Period.

This sounded exactly like my kind of trip. I read Michener's

Caravans and found it thoroughly fascinating. Then, on TV in Los Angeles, I saw a travelogue that followed Michener's book and decided I really wanted to go to Kabul. I discussed it with my Mormon friend, Kay Smith, who said, "We must go before Afghanistan falls to the Russians." How did she get so smart?

I found a trip to Afghanistan in an *Interline Travel* magazine, a KLM Airline special for airline folks only. I called them promptly, only to be told that this specific trip to Afghanistan was not being booked yet, nor were reservations being taken in advance. Not to be deterred, I sent in a reservation form for myself and two of my friends, so KLM would have it in their files when they started making reservations. Lo and behold, my idea worked. We were notified by the Interline Department of KLM that we would be three of the approximately thirty people allowed to be guests of the Government of Afghanistan.

Off we went from Los Angeles to Detroit, to JFK in New York, and to a stopover in Europe before landing in Kabul. We slept whenever and wherever we could, as there was no layover time for rest. We were fitting in this *pleasure* trip between our working trips. We had to do a lot of "trip trading" of our monthly working assignments so that we could take advantage of this much-anticipated adventure. After all, hadn't I let my Spitz dog chew on the ear of the application form that I sent to KLM, so that this application would have a bit of difference and a bit of sense of humor attached to it, and someone would remember it? It was very difficult to book these exotic trips. So many airline people with adventuresome spirits wanted to find and book this very type of trip. Me too!

When we arrived in Kabul, I was very exhausted and excited. We circled over the city on final approach. I could see the red mud hills and mountainous terrain that spread from the local area of the city of Kabul almost to infinity.

Apparently because I was the last person in line to clear Immigration, I was told by the government staff at the Kabul Airport that I *would* be the "Leader" of this group, and I *would* be responsible to see that each member of the group exited from the country as planned. I can see why they wouldn't want an odd American or two to stay behind. This was 1977.

Life Is a Stamp Collection

Later that night, I skipped the reception held for us by the Afghan Tourism Department and hosted by a local official. I would apologize later. I was just too exhausted. By then, we had been up for about forty hours.

The next day, bright and early, our group started by touring that medieval city, Kabul, and its surrounding area. As one fascinating attraction, we were taken to where Genghis Khan had made his headquarters, just outside of Kabul. To get there we had to walk on a high, narrow rock path, which was the top of a ledge open on both sides to only God's air. My friend Sharon informed me this made her dizzy and she was afraid of heights. A flight attendant afraid of heights! So, we held hands, walking sideways, steadying each other while keeping balance and finally arriving at the end of the harrowing wall.

Here the guide regaled us with horrible stories about Genghis Khan. He stated that Genghis Khan could not eat unless he saw human blood flowing in the very street where we were standing. Well, that was charming.

After touring that area, we went back over the stone ledge wall to the bus. As I had been designated the leader of the group, I had to count each time and make sure that no one had defected to the ancient site which we had just visited.

The next day, we flew to Herat to see Afghanistan's historic Buddhas, the ones the Taliban would later blow up in 2000. Before seeing it, we stayed overnight in mud and straw huts called yurts near Bamiyan. Each yurt got twenty minutes of warm running water each day, so when I wanted to wash my hair and bathe, I had to team up with another person. In that mountainous region of Bamiyan, Sharon and I agreed to share the warm running water. We had one rule: we each had to keep our eyes tightly shut and never tell anyone we shared a shower. She dipped in and out of the running water, rinsing off while I scrubbed my head, trying to get the red clay dust out of my blonde hair, and then I would go back under the few seconds of time left to get the cold congealed soap from my scalp. Was this beauty worth it, here in this country where no one bathed anyway, living out in the countryside? Why hadn't Genghis Khan insisted on running water rather than running blood?

We toured the Bamiyan area for a day or two and bought several small carpets, wall hangings, village ladies' wedding boots, and old muskets. A special moment was when Kay, Sharon and I went up the side steps and over the top of the magnificent Buddha. How breathtaking! After we climbed back down, we posed for photos in front of the feet of the Buddha, which were so gigantic that there was no way to capture their magnificence up close. Sadly, I quickly ran out of film and, of course, could not purchase such a commodity in that remote area. It never occurred to me that there were places not modern enough to sell camera film cartridges, even at the foot of the Hindu Kush. Today, readers will laugh that we needed film at all, with digital photography the only way to go in this modern era. But that did not exist back then.

Among my treasured scenes were women with beautiful young children in warm knitted clothes and locally spun wool passing by in camel caravans. Their smiles conveyed, "This is my land, and I am free to be in it, and I love it!" Russians would soon change that attitude.

I stopped one of those caravans and asked the leader if we could photograph them. I was told, "No."

We returned to Kabul for our last night in Afghanistan.

And so, we were soon back on an aircraft flying home, laden with our many purchases. This was one of my primary adventures, and I am so appreciative to have had the opportunity and at that time.

A short time later, the Russians invaded Afghanistan.

Subsequently, a leader of the Afghan revolutionaries, who were fighting the Russians, was in Washington. He met Rusty, a dear girlfriend of mine who worked in the Pentagon during the Reagan Administration. Rusty is one of three sisters who have helped and prayed their friends through many challenges. Rusty told me that when American Airlines changed the uniforms of flight attendants, which airlines do occasionally, we should collect them, with permission. A Washington official, whom Rusty knew, could get the used uniforms to the revolutionaries via Pakistan, near the Afghan border. We were to cut off the buttons that had "AA" on them, so that nothing would appear to show support by any particular corporation or country. I said, "Rusty, how could the skirts of our uniforms do a nomadic freedom-fighter any good?"

She said, "They can stitch up the bottom, put a drawstring at the top and, slung over their backs, use them to carry food."

We put up signs in every operations area of American Airlines and at all the new bases that we flew to and through. Even the Sky Caps' wives were cleaning out their closets of men's clothing and shoes. I wondered how these large-foot-size American shoes would benefit the small-footed Afghan man. Well, I really don't know that their feet were smaller.

With friends that we had recruited, I went to the clothing collection areas of the different AA Bases.

My friend, Sue Woodlee in DFW, helped box the items and, in a coordinated plan, put them on AA flights into Dulles Field. When they arrived almost simultaneously from all bases, many boxes simply burst at the seams. Rusty was there to organize the venture. She told me later, "There was navy blue uniform madness all over the conveyer belts." But being adept at handling such situations, she quickly retrieved the items and had them carted to her basement in Annandale, Virginia.

Along with a hefty sum of cash, the items eventually were transported by Rusty's sister, Dana, to the Afghan border in Pakistan and picked up by the Afghan revolutionaries.

We were told that the bags of navy uniforms, minus AA brass buttons, would be taken into Afghanistan by mules from Pakistan. The journey of the caravan carrying all this "cargo" was done late at night through the mountain passes when the Russian guards would be drunk on cheap vodka. The Russians by this time had quite a foothold in Afghanistan, and the locals did not want them there, as we know.

A few months later, when I was visiting her while enroute for a picture-safari vacation to Kenya, Rusty took me to the basement of her home to show me where the uniform items had rested while she re-packaged them. She said that an official from the Afghan revolutionary army had come to visit her. When she took him to the basement to show him what American flight attendants had collected for his movement, tears came to his eyes.

General Ahmad Shah Massoud said, "I asked Allah for a drink of water, and He has brought me a Coke!"

I would read later; General Ahmad Shah Massoud was not really all that fond of the Americans as he did not trust them.

Sadly, that Afghan was later assassinated during an interview in Afghanistan that was filmed with a video camera made in France. That camera had been stolen nine months earlier from a photojournalist in Grenoble, France. That was Sept. 9th, 2001.

Rusty and her sisters flew for American Airlines. They are strong Catholic ladies. With a bit of help from me and others, they worked diligently to collect funds to build a children's hospital in Afghanistan. The three sisters personally delivered the funds to the people who built the hospital. We understand that it was built, but now I wonder what has become of the place. I do know that the United Nations is working to get cleaner and better facilitated birthing centers for Afghan women in the outlying areas of the country.

The three sisters now live in California after having lived in Annandale, Virginia, for many years. Rodney, the middle sister, took a leave of absence from American Airlines and worked as a liaison for Lenore Annenberg, who was Chief of Protocol in the Reagan Administration.

Rusty married an American-born Jordanian, quit American Airlines, and moved to Amman, Jordan with him. Her marriage ended when "Mike" fell in love with a Lebanese woman he met at a party. Lebanese women were not restricted and could go out among men; Rusty could not, being married to a Muslim Jordanian.

Rusty's husband sent a messenger that said, "I divorce thee, I divorce thee, I divorce thee," three times to her. That was all that was required by Muslim law. I'm sure her heart was crushed though she never used those exact words with me.

Rusty returned to Washington and worked on the Reagan presidential campaign. Later she became an aide to John Harrington, under Secretary of the Navy for Manpower and

Defense. In October 1980, when I was in Washington en route to East Africa, I stopped by to see Rusty and Rodney. She was working under Lenore Annenberg as a special aide for American Airlines. While there, I accompanied Rusty to her office in the Pentagon. She worked while I sat and made conversation with a handsome Marine. I told him I was en route to Nairobi. The Marine asked, "Would you be willing to take a written message to a Marine friend of mine who is stationed in the American Embassy in Nairobi?" I said, "Yes, of course."

Once, Rusty needed to get a picture of a ship framed which would be a gift from John Harrington to an admiral. She called a car and driver, who arrived at the Pentagon, and he opened the doors for us to get in. We were going over to the White House, as the framing department was in the basement. Loved it!

Rusty explained to me that President Nixon had stationed the National Guard in this very basement during the Viet Nam war.

So, after my Washington visit, I flew to New York and took a Pam Am overnight flight to Nairobi. The flight went well, and I arrived at my Nairobi Hotel which had been bombed about two weeks previously.

Kenya, Africa

The Marine's friend turned out to be an aide to the American ambassador to Kenya. The aide was not there. But a nice man said to me that he was the ambassador and asked if he could he give the card to the aide? *Well, yes,* I thought, *that would be fine.* The ambassador invited me to attend a function that night for a US Congressman's son who was there in an aircraft marked Air Force One. The Congressman invited me to ride back to Washington with them if I wished. I cannot believe that I declined. I still had more to do and see in Kenya.

After meeting the ambassador so casually, the next day we went into the countryside to visit the renowned Maasai Mara warrior group.

Here are a few facts about this ancient and respected tribe! The Maasai arrived what is today into central Kenya from the Sudan between 500 to 1,000 years ago. They are one of the best-known ethnic groups living along the Great Rift Valley on arid and semi-arid land. They occupy a total area of 160,000 square kilometers with a total population of half a million people. They live close to nature. They live in mud huts, have no electricity, and no schools.

Everyone eats a lot of meat, beans, avocados, and fruit. There is no rice, which was a first for me, as my dad had been interested in the agricultural expansion of foods which included rice for the starving.

The Maasai cook on a wood fire which is started the Boy Scout way, by rubbing sticks together. The men do the hunting for food, and then the whole village eats together.

Children are not properly acknowledged until they are "three moons" of age because of the high mortality rate. If there is a death, the bodies are left to be eaten by scavengers. If it is not eaten, this brings great shame on the family.

The tribes are the ethnic and semi-nomadic peoples of Kenya and Tanzania, characterized by the bright red dress of the members, which I am sure you have seen in pictures. If not, then please see yours truly with a small boy checking out my flat behind, as the Masai women there have much more pronounced hips.

One of the American women in the group, had a neck scarf on, and a Masai woman seemed quite captivated with it. This American lady was so moved that she took it off and gave it to the Masai woman, feeling connected with that universal feeling that we all share in friendship.

Then the Masai woman turned and tried to sell it to another one of us foreigners. The original giving lady was quite taken aback! Mores are different!

Driving onward, I saw huge satellite dishes standing in a field. I took a picture. Someone said, "Angela, you will take a picture of about anything!"

Well, yes; yes, I will. I never know when an image might be something I'll want to have enlarged as a picture for one of my books, walls, or accent pieces as I arrange various still lifes. When one's life story is not written in the normal life scripts, one must make it be personal, even though it may not be traditional.

Following that, I went by overnight train from Nairobi to Mombasa. The name had always sounded so exotic to me! I paid extra for a mattress bed roll. After finishing my evening snacks, I prepared for sleep. I unrolled the bedding and laid down on it. Soon, roaches were crawling on me and the bed roll mattress.

So, all night, I kept the light on and a house slipper in each hand for hitting a roach as it crawled off the bed roll and me to the walls.

As we approached the African coast of Mombasa, the humidity intensified, making the air very heavy for breathing. I had been in humidity before, for example when we had landed in Bombay returning to India for an assignment. This seemed so much heavier.

I checked into the hotel, went to my room, and there on the dresser was a beautiful basket of fruit. On closer examination, ants had found their way there first.

I took a tour of Mombasa and then went to the Bay. One thing I remember is that in the water one of Onassis's ships that had run aground. I was in a magenta bathing suit, and two men asked if I would like a tour of the water area. Hmm, maybe magenta is my lucky color. They were very adept at managing the boat, but I was not so adept at managing the sun burn.

Chapter Eleven

That PSA Flight

As I crossed the US-Mexico border at the Tijuana crossing on September 25, 1978, I dropped off my little Spitz, Sacha, at a pet boarding location in San Diego. I was enroute to Los Angeles to set off on an adventure on the Trans-Siberian Express! In Los Angeles, I would meet up with two very dear friends, Diana and Dana.

As I drove from San Ysidro, California, on Freeway 805 toward Los Angeles, after crossing the border at Mexico, I played tapes of music on my car's cassette player/stereo. Suddenly, I noticed children and huge oily-looking cloud of smoke billowing outward and upward. I thought, *now where are their mothers, to let their children be so close to a fire? And standing so close to a hill where they could tumble down this hillside onto the freeway!* I can always tell people how to raise children, even though I have none.

I continued toward Los Angeles, all the while listening to my music tapes, never once turning on the radio. My mind was on the anticipated upcoming adventure that awaited us in Russia.

Once I arrived and settled into the LAX airport to await Diana and Dana's arrival, I called my brother, Craig, who resided in the marina area of Los Angeles. He had only recently returned from Viet Nam, where he had been a fixed-wing aircraft pilot. So, being the protective older sister that I am, I was going to help him find a youthful swinging part of LA in which to live, Marina Del Rey.

Craig answered my call with a sound of panic in his voice. "I have been so worried that you could have been on that PSA flight! I knew that you were leaving for Russia today, but I didn't know exactly what route you were traveling to get up here to the airport."

I hadn't a clue what he was talking about. It turned out that at 8:55 a.m., as I was starting north from the border crossing, I was debating which freeway to proceed, the 5 or 805 freeway. My cassette tapes of beautiful music were playing. Life was good. The vehicle traffic looked less dense going up 805, so at the Y where the two freeways split near the US-Mexico border, I proceeded up the 805 freeway.

A Boeing 727 Pacific Southwest Airlines (PSA) commercial aircraft was coming in on final approach to San Diego's Lindbergh Field. The pilots of a Cessna 172, which had flown out of another airfield under a different control tower's command, were unaware that they were coming dangerously close to the PSA.

The rest is history. Later, many months later, the transcript came out in an airline company exam paper. The lines haunt me to this day:

09:01:55 Captain (*in a calm voice*): "Tower, we're going down. This is PSA."

09:01:57 Tower: "OK, we'll get out the (*emergency*) equipment for you."

09:01:58 Sound of stall warning

09:01:59 Captain (*to Tower*) "This is it, baby!"

09:02:03 Captain (*on intercom, to passengers*) "Brace yourself."

PSA Flight 182 struck the ground in a high-speed nose-down attitude, while banked 50 degrees to the right. Seismographic readings indicated that the impact occurred at 09:02:07, about 2.5 seconds after the cockpit voice recorder lost power. The death toll of 144 included all 135 on board PSA

#182, plus the two men aboard the Cessna and seven people on the ground, including a family of four. Nine others on the ground were injured and twenty-two homes were destroyed or damaged.

    I had just passed the site as the black smoke billowed from the burning airplane fuel. Black smoke indicates there was plenty of fuel; grey smoke indicates the aircraft was running out of fuel.

    Later at our bi-yearly FAA exams, I was able to read the conversation between the control tower and the doomed airplane cockpit. I just remember hearing/reading the control tower air traffic controller say, after the captain had explained that he had been hit, "Roger, Captain, we will send equipment." So hollow. Everyone in the control tower and in the cockpit knew the comment was just a useless and mind-numbing sad statement. Once again, I had been so close but totally protected from a horrible disaster. Nothing fell on the freeway, and I was oblivious to the collision that had happened above me.

Chapter Twelve

A Holiday Trip through Russia

In 1978, I was living in Punta Bandera, Baja Mexico, on the cliffs above the Pacific Ocean. It's about half an hour south of Tijuana, on the toll road going toward Roserito Beach and eventually ending up in Cabo San Lucas. An American man named the town Roserito Beach. He did not realize that Spanish words have gendered endings.

Exquisite azure water was my front yard. The dolphins played occasionally where I could view their water calisthenics from my terrace of white marble chips, with pots of overhanging magenta bougainvillea.

The sights were simply the "Gifts of the Gods." The peace of nature is something we all take for granted, and how fortunate was I to experience this after my "gaslight marriage" to Albert Edinger of Redondo Beach.

Out of that location, I commuted from SAN to LAX to work my trips. Usually, after driving up from Baja, I parked at the San Diego airport and then flew thirty minutes as a passenger from San Diego to Los Angeles to LAX.

As I was always in uniform and as I drove through the Tijuana-US Border control point, sometimes my trips took me from LAX to Toronto, Canada, (YYZ) it meant that I was in three countries all in one day. Would that fact make me sound like

I could be in some nefarious activities? Three countries in one day? So, I just always told the truth, but no more than that.

Now, without uniform, I drove to Los Angeles, not to work a flight, but to join up with my LAX friends and fellow flight attendants, Diana and Dana. We were meeting up with Dana's friend, Marge, from New Zealand. That would make four of us. We were to leave on Pan Am to start out on our adventure to fly to Japan's Haneda Airport and then go by train to Yokohama.

Sometime later I learned that the Haneda airport was the one the US forces bombed during World War II.

In Japan, we connected with Marge and proceeded out of Yokohama across the Sea of Japan on a Russian steamer. As we approached the Russian steamer, colorful flags were flapping in the breeze of this beautiful ship.

We crossed the Japanese sea to arrive at Nakhodka, Russia. Then as the guidebooks stated, we were to "travel in the cars of the Tsars, from the west coast of Russia to Moscow, across the Ural Mountains and through Siberia! The walls will be lined with polished cherry wood, and the brass railing will be gleaming with perfection!"

Um, I don't think so. But I digress.

We boarded our Trans-Siberian Express train and had two compartments for the four of us. It seemed that we would be sharing one between-compartment bathroom. At our connecting stopover, we talked with a very nice English-speaking gentleman. We explained that we had requested an attached bath for each compartment. He listened and assured us that would be the case onward.

Well, not exactly ...

As we continued, there was only one latrine at the very end of the train car for everyone. It consisted of a hole in the flooring, thank you, and a sink with cold water.

So much for our request for individual car loos.

The other train was luxurious by these standards, but little did we know how we would survive this ordeal as Americans who had actual toilet seats on their commodes. And so, this is remembered now with a chuckle, of sorts. I read once that diplomats, when visiting Moscow, had one toilet seat amongst them which they passed around. How true is this? Who knows? Perhaps now there is no need for the "traveling toilet seat" for American diplomats.

We found that all Russian train stations keep a large clock on the exterior of the main building. The time is always kept on Moscow time.

We had to book this trip through "Intourist," which was the only way to book the Trans-Siberian Express. We had to pay for all our meals in advance, and after eating in the dining car for several meals, we knew that we would need to come up with a better way to survive. Also, the cook and several others sold our meal components/rations to local townspeople along the way at stopovers. Some of the crew kept frozen sturgeon/fish in a compartment under the floor of the train corridor car, which they would sell to us, if we wanted. We didn't.

As the train wandered onward, there were still a few things we needed to do to survive as travelers. One was when the train stopped, we four would get off and each had an assignment, as food-for-sale tables were set up at all the stations. One went for the sugar water. *Yes, it really is a thing.* One went for the boiled-egg stand, one went for cookies, etc. I always travel with peanut butter so that gave us a little protein.

Our train stewardess was named Svetlana, the same name as Stalin's daughter. She burst in quite often, and if we were taking a picture, she gaily would take the camera from our hands and look into the eye to see of what we were taking a picture. There was always a helicopter which hovered and followed us as we were a "tourist train."

There were some Russian soldiers on this train, and they mingled with some of the foreigners. One traveling group was with an American Express leader/escort. In our case we were basically on our own mixed in with others, including some Israelis. We became friendly and would say the occasional "hello" to each other in the train corridor.

Then, there was an incident which still brings me pause. The Russian soldiers had been reported by the American Express tour leader, and they were taken off at a scheduled stop in the middle of Siberia.

We were so shocked! That evening, I stepped out into the corridor to breathe a bit of fresh air from an open window. The train was always so over-heated.

I saw a lady sitting at the other end of the car, sitting, doing exactly what I wished to do. I started to go and ask her if she had heard anything about the Russian soldiers' removal. But then cautionary hesitation proved to be my friend. I knew her to be the American Express tour leader. I later found out that this very lady with no Russian accent had turned in the unsuspecting soldiers. She was the Intourist Soviet spy!

We continued onward, and several times we pulled over to a side rail to let many cars pass with Russian Army equipment.

Passing through the Ural Mountains was a delight for me as they have a very romantic lore, which I had read. We would have been going thru the Ural Mountains at night if the Russian Military trains had not taken precedence over tourist trains.

Once in the middle of the trip, we stopped in a Siberian town, and we four took a tour to a Russian Orthodox Catholic church. It was like out of a movie for central casting. Russian priests walked around with wonderful long black orthodoxy robes. They also had tall, great hats on.

To my left, a group of shriveled-up elderly ladies sat all in a row, dressed in black, not doing anything but perhaps just waiting to die. This passed the time for them, I suppose. Men dressed in suits held briefcases and just stood there, pretending not to be doing surveillance in the middle of the church. Intimidation!

Soon it was time to return to our hotel.

We stayed in Irkutz, a city in the Eastern Gateway to Siberia, for a few days, and then we chose to continue our train journey. We found people to be rude to us as soon as they heard our American accent. However, we just kept on seeing the beauty in their buildings, or the lack thereof.

There were two student-like young people in uniforms by an Eternal Flame, occasionally passing off a rifle to each other.

Lake Baikal is a massive ancient lake in the mountainous region of Siberia, north of the Mongolian border. It is the deepest lake in the world and is quite famous for being the oldest freshwater lake in the world, estimated to be 25 million years old. It is circled by a network of hiking paths called the Great Baikal Trail and is 1,496 feet above sea level. It was formed in an ancient rift valley. It is 397 miles long by 50 miles wide; 336 rivers flow into the lake, and one flows out. It is stated that it holds more water than all the North American Great Lakes.

It was once claimed that you could drink the water right out of the lake, but now sewage is being dumped into it, and there is contamination around all sides of the lake. It gets green algae just like we do in our Florida canals and in the Gulf water. If emptied, it would take over 359 years to refill it!

While continuing onward, we spent more time over on the side rails for letting the military-trains bypass us. My friends smoked, we danced Cossack style in the corridor, arm in arm, moving sideways. A little vodka was had by a few of us.

Finally, we arrived in Moscow. Once we exited, we walked from the Terminal to meet our local tour guide. After meeting him, he berated us for being so late for our arrival! Is this something Russian, not knowing the facts but blaming the Americans quickly?

We checked into our hotel. Later we went to the dining room for a meal. They handed us a menu with about fifty items. However, we would soon learn that there were only about eight items that we could order. If we asked a question, the waitresses mocked our American English, and acted most indignant. We were so demoralized about the behavior, and it was such a disappointment for the welcome to Moscow.

We shopped in a foreign currency store where we had to pay in US dollars. Russians always wanted hard currency. A lady came in wearing a babushka, and you could tell she was not a lady of means, as there was a naïve innocence about her. She was promptly escorted out, and we continued buying Russian tea glasses with silver filigree holders, etc. You know, not that any of this is monumental, but many, many years later, when I worked trips to Tokyo (NRT) on American Airlines, I was told AA paid $20,000 to fly through Russian airspace for about twenty minutes. That is how much paying for a shorter route saves fuel for AAL. Russia gets hard currency, and we burn less fuel!

While we were there, these little Russian boys followed us everywhere. They never begged, so I was never sure if it was just curiosity or if they were looking for handouts. One carried a little kitten in his arms the whole time.

Stalin's Only Daughter

A bit of history that was later of interest to me.

Svetlana Iosefavna Alliluyeva was Stalin's only daughter, born to his second wife whose last name was Alliluyeva. This was on Feb. 28, 1926.

Svetlana seemed oblivious to her father's history of annihilating nine million Russians. She was the darling of Stalin's eye. Stalin's name for her was "little sparrow."

After she grew up in a very pampered lifestyle, she fell in love several times, but Stalin sent them all away. One man was sent to a forced labor camp in Siberia. So that was not to be. Stalin still hated this man when he returned nineteen years later. Even though the young man had been sent to Siberia for years, Stalin showed no remorse for upsetting his daughter's life.

Somewhere during all this, Stalin's son was captured by the Germans and when they offered a trade for his son to get back one of their generals, Stalin said "No." His son was then executed by the Germans.

One of Svetlana's lovers was an Indian communist from the Georgia-Russia area. Kunwar Brajesh Singh and Svetlana were both ill and met on the Black Sea and recuperated at Sochi. Once again, her father did not approve of him. When Kunwar died, Svetlana asked permission to take his ashes to India to put in the Ganges. The Yamuna is the river which flows by Delhi and eventually into the Ganges.

Svetlana was given rare permission by one of the Russian higher up politicians to travel to Delhi. She then flew to New Delhi, with Kunwar Brajesh Singh's ashes, which I assume she put into the Yamuna.

Then, Svetlana went to the American Embassy, which had been designed by an Arkansas architect, and presented herself to our undercover CIA officer and asked for asylum in America. I don't believe this was an entirely impulsive act.

It just so happened that the American Ambassador was Chester Bowles, from my New Delhi days when I was ten, waiting to go to Nepal.

He notified Washington of this conundrum and stated he wanted to get her out of the embassy as soon as he could. He then put her, in the middle of the night, on a plane into Rome.

As a side note here, prior to that my mother was talking with the man Svetlana defected to. We will call him "Jim." Mother said that she mentioned to Jim regarding the time he lived in Tehran. Jim, said to Mother that he had never lived in Tehran. Mother argued with him and said, "I know you said you did."

The telephone went dead. As soon as that happened, Mother knew immediately someone had been monitoring the telephone lines, whether the American Embassy or the Indians by another surveillance method. They were on the phone together, yes, and the lines went through the Embassy switch board, for the Americans.

So, "Jim" appeared immediately at my parents' front door, and he stated that the information was highly confidential, which my mother immediately understood.

With my mother talking about Jim's past record and with Svetlana defecting, Jim was told to leave Delhi for a different assignment, I suppose, as he was no longer a part of that conclave of Americans.

Svetlana arrived in the States. She wrote books, and they brought in a nice sum of money, which she did not save but spent readily. She had always had a very nice life with Stalin as her father, and I presume she thought it should continue.

In 1970, she met and married an acolyte of Frank Lloyd Wright, William Wesley Peters, and they lived in Arizona. A girl child was born. They named her Olga Peters. She later changed her name to Chrese Evans and moved to Portland, Oregon.

A quote from Anais Nin seems appropriate. "And the day came when the risk to remain tight in a bud was more painful than to risk what it took to blossom."

Chapter Thirteen

A Flight Attendant's Worst Nightmare

May 25, 1979 was a day when I didn't have to work. I spent much of the morning outside my beautiful little pink casa in Mexico, planting flowers in clay pots, relishing the beauty that only sunshine on the Pacific can bring. Then, I went inside to prepare lunch for myself and Sacha, my naughty little loveable white Spitz, an American Eskimo dog.

Because my house sat on a cliff overlooking the crashing waves, it had a direct line of focus to Point Loma in San Diego from which I could get reception for a few American stations on my Sony TV. When I turned on the TV, there was a special bulletin: an American Airlines DC 10 jet had crashed at Chicago's ORD airport. An engine had fallen off the left wing, and the plane had plummeted from the sky! Crew members' names rolled down the screen. My legs went numb. My heart breaks now, just from the memory.

So far, I recognized only one name, Kathy Heibert, and I did not know her well. But two names were not listed, pending notification of next of kin. To no avail, I stayed tuned in all day and all night to my only English language connection with the outside world, hoping to know who the other two flight attendants were.

The next day, I had to work a trip out of LAX (Los Angeles). I drove through Tijuana to the San Diego airport and parked "The Thing," my little Volkswagen jeep, near the airport bus stop. While I waited for the bus, some San Diego-based flight attendants whom I knew came by. One of them asked, "Have you heard about the AA # 191 flight that had 'gone in' at Chicago?"

"Yes," I said, my voice cracking with trepidation. "Do you know who the other two flight attendants were?"

"Carmen Fowler and …"

I didn't hear the other name above my controlled, muffled screams. The screams resounded in my mind. I'm not sure if they came out of my mouth. I had to get control, though my heart was so sad. When our hearts are broken, I think God puts our hearts into His outstretched hand. Flight attendants are not to show emotions about these things, especially when we are going to work. The San Diego flight attendants remained calm, and I suppose they were as much in shock as were most other employees of American Airlines. Certainly, the passengers' families—indeed, the entire nation—were in shock. Flight AA #191 remains the deadliest single aircraft accident in US history. The 9/11/01 tragedy, of course, was NOT an accident.

Carmen's name had not been on the TV screen because they were unable to locate her estranged husband, who was considered her next of kin.

DC 10s were grounded for several weeks. Meanwhile, American Airlines offered paid leaves of absence. *Would my plane be next*? Rather than walk around and speculate whether I would be next, as I'm sure all flight crews did, I decided to take leave and do some traveling further into the interior of Mexico. I would feel safe there.

Whenever I was in a small village, I would go into one of their beautiful crude yet picturesque, Catholic churches and just sit calmly and feel the desire for the peace and my heart to heal. I felt close to Carmen in Catholic churches. She was Catholic and, although she had lived in San Diego, she was Mexican-American.

I soon felt a responsibility to know when American Airlines would start flying the DC 10s again. So, while in the interior of Mexico, I watched for news. One evening I heard that Congress had ungrounded the DC 10. I called from a phone booth outside the Guadalajara bus station to get Crew Schedule in LAX. Diesel fumes and other odors gagged me as I shouted into the pay phone to Crew Schedule, "Do I need to return for flights on the DC 10?"

The answer: "No. It is still grounded."

"But Walter Cronkite said Congress had ungrounded it!"

I was starting to be asphyxiated from the diesel fumes, and it was hard to hear above the bus horns and shouting children. However, I felt that if Walter Cronkite said that Congress had … well, you know, I had best get back up to the States.

Eventually, the issues with the DC 10 were resolved, and we got back to life as it had been before. If *as it had been before* is ever really possible.

The DC 10 was a great aircraft. It was so unfortunate that circumstances happened which made the left engine fall off on takeoff out of ORD on that fateful day. I shall never forget my wonderful friend who was always cheering me on when I would be down over the impending break-up of one of my life's events.

Carmen and I had become very good friends, and I will miss her forever. One time we decided to do some skiing together. We were both separated from our husbands at the time. Her pilot husband had decided he needed "space" and had gone to live between trips with some single fellows on Catalina Island.

On one of our days off, Carmen and I flew up to Mammoth and then hitchhiked with other skiers over to June Lake, California. Those were the days when skiing was wholesome and safe. People were wonderful to look out for each other.

That night a most magnificent snowfall—several feet— came while we were asleep. The next day, I skied the most heavenly runs that I have ever experienced on powder. Carmen loved the skiing as well. The powder smoothed our glides down the mountainsides, and it felt like we were descending in slow motion through a fairyland. Memories like this of my dear friend will live with me forever.

Chapter Fourteen

Layover Cities

Casablanca

In the late 1970s, my friend Sharon and I were in Casablanca. This was a "busman's holiday," not a layover, as American Airlines did not fly there. I inquired about "doing a camel caravan." Doing a camel caravan? Now, does that sound like a person who has traveled too much? We two had survived an Afghanistan trip, so Morocco sounded like a piece of cake.

I asked Baby, the driver we had hired in Casablanca, what he knew about these caravans. He said, "The Germans come here all the time to go on caravans."

"Could you arrange for me to go on one?" I asked.

He said "Oh, yes, of course."

Then I asked, "Where would I sleep?"

"Where would you want to sleep? With the *womens* or the *mens*?"

I am sure the look of confusion on my face said it all. "Well, with the women, of course."

"When the German *womens* come, they want to sleep with the *mens*. In the men's part of the nightly encampment."

I didn't want to sound like a prude, but I cancelled the

camel caravan.

Sharon and I took a side trip to Fez and had a delightful tour of greater historic information. Fez had been the capitol of Morocco twice.

That night we took a bus back to Casablanca. We were the only women, both American, one of blond, one brunette. We took the only seats left, the two remaining in the very back. I could watch the forward part of the van, and all wore hooded djellabas. I watched the hoods sway in unison with the curves of the road. So interesting, I thought as we were on this adventure deep in this exotic land. Not so profound, but to me it was a new experience.

Charles Lindbergh

With flying in my blood, the story of Charles Lindbergh has always fascinated me. On April 15, 1926, he flew as an American Airways pilot from St. Louis to Chicago. This was the first flight to carry US mail. American Airways was started in 1930 via a union of more than eighty small airlines. The two organizations from which American Airlines originated were Robertson Aircraft Corporation and Colonial Air Transport. This was made into an operating company in 1930 and rebranded as American Airways.

Lindbergh's flight from St. Louis to Chicago followed directional ground cement blocks with white arrows painted on them, pointing out the route. This was the origin of air as the most expeditious way to deliver written communication. Over the ocean, of course, painted guidance blocks would not work. I was told by a retired AA pilot, Barry Brannan, that radio beacons along with flashing lights with code for nighttime were the norm.

On June 15, 1919, the first nonstop flight over the Atlantic Ocean was done by two men named Alcock and Brown. In May 1927, the first solo flight across the Atlantic was done by Charles Augustus Lindbergh. He landed at Le Bourget Field in Paris. He reported that he ate only 1 ½ sandwiches as he flew across in

33 ½ hours. He was the nineteenth person to cross the Atlantic but the first to fly it solo. His aircraft was named "The Spirit of St. Louis." This plane was designed by Donald Hall under the direct supervision of Charles Lindbergh. It was a highly modified version of a conventional RYAN M-2 strut-based monoplane powered by a reliable 223 p Wright J-5C engine.

As I researched information regarding the first flight, I found that Russia and India, with their designs, made claims to have been the first to fly.

Honolulu

Once when I was working in first class on a 747, a man called me over and said, "Go and ask the man in 2B if he is Charles Lindbergh." He was not. However, he looked back and saw it was another passenger putting me up to this slight embarrassment, and he waved to him.

I was offered a stay in a condo on Maui, and that was just what I needed to uncurl the kinks of flying too many all-nighters to Honolulu. I went over for a few days and just slept and slept some more, with my windows open to the wonderful Hawaiian air.

I decided to take a guided tour around the island and asked if they would be stopping near Lindbergh's grave. The tour guide said the family had asked that it not be included on their tours. But, after I explained that I was an AA flight attendant of the airline Lindbergh helped establish, he said that he would drop me off. He did.

I walked down a dirt path which passed a small quaint church named Palapala Ho'omau Church which was built in 1857. It still stands along Maui's lush coastline near to Lindbergh's elevated grave covered with lava stone. It made a special tug in my heart, and I have never forgotten the nice tour guide who made an exception for my meaningful experience.

Chapter Fifteen

Michael Summers

Michael John Summers, is an Englishman to whom I was briefly engaged in 1985. Briefly, I say, since once I was asked to get married, I immediately started feeling like, "How can I get out of this?"

English men would say to their wives something like, "My dear, just lie back and think of England." So, in the stifling monsoon heat of Simla, India, or even down in the Terrai, I am sure that many a British child was conceived for the glory of England.

Michael and I were not destined to have a life together, even though I had hoped for that. He and I met on the airplane and became familiar through a few phone calls, etc. The more I got to know Michael John, handsome though he might be, the leerier I became. He did not use credit cards. Or pay his bills on time. I always tried to keep up my spirits after my evaluations of him. He was an adventurer and in the gold mining business in the Las Vegas area. I felt he could understand my crazy childhood. He lived off an expense account provided by his English partner/boss, who lived there as well. The boss had a mistress, Gemma, who came out from London and spent time there in Boulder City, outside of Las Vegas.

I thought, since my life was so different than most,

perhaps he just was going through a rough patch. Michael had overseen the building of a dam Queen Elizabeth had given to the country of Ceylon (now known as Sri Lanka).

I lived in Boulder City with Michael and my dog, Sacha, for a few months and commuted to Dallas to work my trips.

Later when I moved back to La Costa, CA with Sacha in tow, Michael came along as the gold mining business had not been kind to his boss's investments.

Finally, I realized that this relationship was not going to work out. I tried to work and juggle taking care of my home in Baja, Mexico, and my home in La Costa, and commute to Dallas to work my trips for AA.

Somewhere in there we went to England.

We went sailing on the river Thames near Henley. In the middle of the river, I asked Michael if he would be willing to sign a pre-nuptial agreement if we got married. When he failed to answer in a timely manner, I stumbled about verbally, saying since my brother was a lawyer, I thought it was for his own protection. I had my answer though, didn't I?

Another time he told me that he had wanted to buy his son a used car, and he was bemoaning the fact that he did not have the money. I asked if he wanted me to loan it to him.

"Yes, please." He stated that he would send money back from England to reimburse me. He did, but his money order bounced twice at Bank of America in La Joya.

I just wanted him out of my life. One less thing to have to support. My loneliness was intense for me at the point of meeting him in flight, and so I made choices that at least let me know that I had tried to make my decision work. I told God that I had tried to make every opportunity work, but it just was not to be.

Savoring Egypt's History

In 1985, my friend Gwen and I decided to go on vacation to Egypt. We would visit three special cities: Cairo, Luxor, and Aswan.

Life Is a Stamp Collection

The last time I had been to Egypt was with my family when I was ten years old. It was a brief stopover in 1952 when we were on our way to India. We had landed in Cairo near nightfall and would have an early departure to Baghdad the next morning. My father immediately arranged a taxi to take us to Giza where we rode camels and saw the Sphinx and the Pyramids. My brother, sister and I rode camels in the fading sunlight on sand. It was my first time to see so much sand. I had seen the beautiful Arkansas soil but never sand.

My camel was named Seven Up. Since I was only ten, I didn't realize that I was being exposed to American capitalism indirectly. I just thought the name Seven Up was wonderfully familiar, there at the base of these fabulous historical creations, which I would soon study in my Calvert homeschool system in Kathmandu.

I did not appreciate the history on this particular visit as much as my parents did. We children were so tired and sleepy from our plane ride from Paris to Cairo. It seems that my father wanted his children to see these collective wonders of the world, even if he were just as exhausted as my siblings and me.

With these memories as a blur, Gwen and I chose to visit the fascinating country of Egypt. There are very few cities or countries that I desire to revisit, as I have had the good fortune to experience wonderful opportunities to ingest thoroughly exquisite adventures in the countries of my choice. But Aswan is one of those places on earth in which I would jump in a second to go back for an exotic Agatha Christie-type of setting. There the air was clear, and the clean beige sand was ever so bright and glistening. The sea was exquisite in its turquoise, shimmering beauty. It was breathtaking!

At sundown every day on our stay, a few *falupas,* Egyptian sail boats with their white sails, would move slowly in the breezes. As we sat on the veranda of the Aswan Hotel, we were mesmerized by the beauty of the seaside. I kept wondering if it were okay for us to be there. It seemed right out of a Hollywood movie setting, either Agatha Christie or *Lawrence of Arabia.*

From there we traveled to Luxor where there were so many details that I could not remember them all, even with the photos I took. I studied them for hours after returning to my home in La Costa, California.

All too soon, it was time to return to Cairo for a few more hot but profound days. I found Cairo to be a very difficult city in which to get around. The heavy traffic plus construction on the main streets and roads kept us in gridlock. One misses a lot unless one has days and days to move around in the city.

I chose not to go on an out-of-town excursion with the rest of my traveling group. Instead, with the help of an English-speaking driver, I asked to visit the Cairo Museum and a Coptic church. Alas, we sat in traffic for so long waiting to move a few inches I canceled the Museum and decided to revisit a special church. It had been on our sightseeing tour a few days before the trip to Aswan, and I was drawn to see it again. After seeing it the first time, I wanted to go back and experience the feeling of its history.

We finally arrived at the small grounds of St. Sargius Church, which has the distinction of being the "oldest church in Egypt." It was also claimed that this is the place "where the Holy Family lived for some time during their stay in Egypt."

The host, Reverend Gabriel G. Bestavros, was the priest of the church. He explained the story something like this: "When the Holy Family was fleeing harm's way, they were given refuge in this location now named St. Sargius Church. The Holy Family stayed in what is now called "The Crypt of the Holy Family."

An orphanage was adjacent to the church on the same small property. In a window of one of the buildings, we could see Reverend Bestavros's wife sewing. From there, she could see the children playing on a small playground. I felt that I was truly in a place of genuineness.

The reverend and I walked down a few steps in the direction of the crypt. We could only go so far, as water seeps from the Nile into the lower basement area and, occasionally, covers some of the steps. As I stood on the steps, just above the water line, looking into the dark area of the crypt, a special feeling of truth washed over me. There was such a knowing. It was so personal.

I am one of the most skeptical people about the several places where it is claimed that Christ was buried in the Holy Land or where the different tourist sites offer for sale the relics of saints. Visiting the crypt in Cairo was indeed a reassuring, introspective experience, especially compared with the falsity of self-proclaimed religious pundits or Hollywood films. I have always felt that too many people choose not to be in charge of their own responsibility for the dogma in which they believe.

I asked the kind-hearted priest if he needed anything special.

He replied, "Well, if you would like to buy one of the tin Coptic crosses that the children make to sell to the people who come here, because of our history, I would be happy."

Indeed, I bought one. I also left him with the remainder of my traveler's checks. I knew that his need was greater than my need for yet *another* alabaster bowl.

As I left the priest and the Coptic Church, I was so pleased that I had been able to have this wonderful afternoon, alone, without the distraction of others.

Soon, the driver was navigating the afternoon traffic, shouting at those who drove just like he. As the horns honked and voices blared, I silently reflected on how special those people are, who cross our paths at the will of the Universe. I shall never forget St. Sargius Church or Rev. Bestavros and his wife and what they were giving to make a better future for part of the next generation of Egyptians.

That Coptic cross, together with a picture of Christ and a picture of a young Buddhist Monk that I photographed on a trip to a Buddhist temple in Narita, Japan, adorn my very private little alter at my home in Marco Island, Florida. These are symbols of my gratitude for the wonderful life that I have been presented by Divine Providence.

Chapter Sixteen

Father's Close Call

In 1991, on an icy day in Memphis, Tennessee, my flight was one of the last American Airlines 727 jets to circle through the dense clouds to land safely and taxi to the terminal. The ice storm had shut down many Tennessee towns as well as the Memphis airport, after I landed.

I had traveled from San Diego on the unexpected news of my father's heart attack. We had never known of any problem with my father's heart.

I sat by his bed the night before his planned surgery. I just let him talk. He noted that the feeling of him being held and rocked lovingly as a child was still with him, as his mother died when he was three months old. He still felt that loving gesture, seventy years later.

Shortly, his thoughts and discussion went to his work in the Foreign Service. He described how more people were eating better than when he had first gone to Nepal in 1952. In addition to Nepal, his work overseas had included Bangkok, Thailand, and tours in two different areas in India.

When he was in Thailand, he gave a speech at "Sala Santitham," in Bangkok to SEATO on Community Development July 1965.

As Daddy reminisced, I somehow had a haunting feeling that this could be our last conversation. He drifted off in that cold room while the ice storm outside demanded that the emergency generators work at maximum capacity. I sat huddled in my camel-wool coat. At one point, a nurse walked in and asked why I looked so worried. I explained that my father was very ill. She said that the test the next morning was simply routine, and there was nothing to worry about, but something inside me felt differently.

Weakness was never a trait to be exhibited by the Sanders family. And being the eldest of four children in a Foreign Service family, I would show none now.

One of my brothers, Roger, finally made it into Memphis from Dallas. The following day we were called into the holding room beside the operating theatre to see my father before his surgery. It was there that we were told that my father had a 50% chance of making it through the surgery per his physicians' educated opinions. We learned that his upper aorta was ripping. Our family's lives had never followed a safe, uncurious path. Ever.

Apparently, the findings were such that during the routine test they had immediately stopped. As they explained, they were assembling the best heart team in Memphis. My brother and I waited in the Critical Care waiting room. A call came indicating that Daddy would not make it through the surgery.

I immediately visualized my father in perfect health with his granddaughters, Arden, Rebecca, and Alexis, playing at his feet. I placed him in a setting of sunshine and the beautiful sounds of nature. I felt his mother's presence with us, the mother who had died when my father was just three months old. I prayed that this man, who had done so much for others, would be looked after in the most Divine way.

I told God that we would find new ways to be compatible as a family — just give us more time with Daddy.

My brother, Roger, decided to talk about the Baylor Bears and their scoring stats.

I kept visualizing while listening to Roger. I pictured the

sunshine peeping through the leaves and casting warmth on the love being exhibited by his three granddaughters.

A long thirty minutes later, we received a call from the nurse: "Your father is resting in recovery and will be wheeled into the Intensive Care Unit shortly."

WOW! Perhaps visualizing and Baylor Bears, was a winning combination: I say, who knew?

Revisit to Ellerslie Villa

In 1991, after I had been married for a time and divorced, I revisited Ellerslie Villa with my Auckland House boarding school girlfriend, Rana Sundar Singh, now, Rana Gurdip Singh.

I was invited to join some Sikh friends on a *shikar*. A *shikar* is a lion hunt on elephant-back. Originally I said I would *think* about it but declined.

The owner of the Ellerslie Villa, where we had lived in 1955-1957, graciously invited me to stay in the home at any time. In return, I invited her to visit me in Florida.

Health Concerns

My first serious health issue came in 1964 — cancer of the thyroid. Doctors successfully removed it, and I had radiation.

All went well until 1992 when I had a melanoma removed from the bottom of my right great toe. Again, it was not a bad cancer. I called it "one of the better versions" of melanoma. Superficial spreading, the cancer had not penetrated too deeply. Then, two brain tumors were removed — one in 1996 and the other in 2003. Benign, thank heavens!

After the latter experience, I decided that even if I could not afford to retire, I would call it quits after being a flight attendant for forty years. In addition to the possible exposure to radiation that I had on a dairy farm in Arkansas, radiation in the air was greatest over the route to Japan that I choose to fly and that I enjoyed so much.

On layovers in Japan, I would go to a great Buddhist Temple and sit at the very back, so as not to draw too much attention to my fair hair and skin. It was so healing for me. Today, I call myself a Christian Buddhist. Buddhism is a religion about 600 years older than Christianity, and it has some of the same gentle laws or tenants as Christianity's Ten Commandments

As a kid in Nepal, my father helped start church services at one of the palaces where we lived. We would often picnic at the base of Buddhist stupas, after our service. We kids ran around irreverently, whirling the temple's prayer wheels. I guess that is why I believe so much in mind over matter and connecting with the great healing powers of the Universe.

Ruptured Appendix in Japan

During our descent in a Boeing 777 into Narita, Japan, in the spring of 2000, I didn't feel so well. I was queasy. I began to regret that I had eaten that meal of Japanese fish an hour before.

After all passengers had departed the plane and the cockpit crew was standing in the first-class aisle, all the strength ebbed from my body. I thought, *I must be exhausted from working a full twelve-hour flight.* I struggled trying to lift my suitcase packed with enough clothing, food, and books for the layover. I so wanted to ask one of the crew to help me. However, with the advent of women's lib, we ladies knew we were to carry our own weight, so to speak, as this was what we had fought for. Cockpit crew members are very considerate men, and I in no way demean them.

I finally got through customs and immigration and arrived outside the terminal at our crew bus. I made it to my room at the Tokyu Inn hotel on the outskirts of Narita. The next morning, still not feeling chipper, I went to our "Airline Crew Only" cafeteria and ordered a nice US Southern-type breakfast of scrambled eggs, bacon, toast, and juice. This always helps, having familiar food when one is out of the country continuously. I watched industrious crewmembers playing tennis right outside the restaurant window.

After finishing the large breakfast, I did the usual. I went to the main lobby to rent a computer for 100 *yen*. I checked company e-mail, inbound equipment arrival times, and to see if there were any changes to my schedule. Thank goodness, no changes.

Now, the decision was whether I felt like going to the Buddhist temple, catching the bus right outside the hotel, or going back to rest in my room. I decided to go to my room. As I entered the room, I started to lose consciousness.

As consciousness waxed and waned, I recalled the time when a policeman, who had been shot and while dying, wrote in the palm of his hand the license of the car he had been pursuing.

As consciousness returned to me, I wrote down in a pad all the events and phone numbers of such that I had booked for the next few days after my scheduled return to the States. In case I was really sick, they could be cancelled by my friend when she returned to the States.

I called my friend Marilyn Eacker, Bill Cherry's love, and asked if she could help. She called one of the Japanese speakers assigned to our flight, Jeff Hiskey, and asked if he would help in this emergency. He said that he could not as he was cataloging his CDs.

The front desk at the Tokyu Inn called a taxi for us, and soon we were off to the hospital, with every bump jarring the jagged pain which was unfolding in my body. We arrived. I was soon admitted to a Red Cross hospital where most foreigners, including people on inbound flights, were taken.

Marilyn procured a wheelchair, came back to the back seat and somehow, I got out and into the rolling chair. As I was pushed over the bumpy cobblestones and through the hospital doors, a lady in a nurse's white uniform asked if she could help.

Marilyn must have explained that I was in unendurable pain, as I was going in and out of consciousness. The following picture is imbedded in my memory: a row of Japanese patients waiting, and I was bypassing them! Japanese people were so polite, and here I was being rude bypassing them.

The staff at the hospital spoke no English, and they didn't

want to make a decision about what was wrong with me. They packed me in ice and laid me on a stone bed. It was the most excruciating pain I have ever known. My white blood cell count was off the charts.

Later, freezing, and so much in pain, I lay in a bed in a hospital where there was no heat. I started to drift out of my body. I pulled myself back and focused on the white clouds painted on the walls, where the lights coming in from the nighttime of businesses like McDonalds were reflected. I thought, *how nice it was of the Japanese to paint clouds on the walls in case a child should be sick in this room.* I would realize later that they were not clouds but plaster missing due to the many earthquakes.

As I was drifting, I thought, *Whoa! Stay in the here and now, and just talk to God.* I decided then that if I made it through this sickness, I would go home and start living my dreams. I would find a way to build a house on my empty lot on Marco Island and, well, I would just find a way. I am always protected, and I am always blessed

The hospital staff decided that I had peritonitis from a ruptured appendix. They set about to get American Airlines permission to treat me. They called my brother, Roger, in Texas to get a family member's permission, and they asked my permission. What did I have to lose?

They saved my life.

With the help of an American Airlines supervisor who spoke English and Japanese, the Airline flew my sister Brenda over to help take care of me.

A lovely Japanese lady, Reiko Tachibano, was in the hospital awaiting a surgery for a mastectomy, and she overheard the nurses saying that there was a lady who had been admitted and who only spoke English. Reiko volunteered to translate between the Japanese doctors and me. At some point Reiko came into my room and explained that she spoke English and would be happy to help. What a godsend!

As I was recovering, I was made to walk up and down the halls. Japanese ladies would lean forward in their beds to gander at this *gaijin*, or foreigner, who was so weird looking with yellow hair. Then, just as I got to their location, they quickly looked away, so as to be polite.

Every evening as I lay shivering under comforters, I could hear beautiful caroling music floating over the town. As the notes played at exactly at six p.m., I knew another day has passed. Or was this just the same music replaying in my mind? Sounds drifted in and out of my ears as I struggled to stay conscious.

I was told later the words to this song:

> *Little children, it is time for you to be home,*
> *safe in the protective*
> *arms of your parents and family.*
> *Little children you are loved.*
> *Return to your embracing family now.*

When Reiko visited me in Florida, she brought a small music box that played this very song.

I noticed green seepage coming out of my wound area, which made circles behind my back and left shoulder and was spreading upwards. The pump to remove the gangrene must have been malfunctioning, but at the time, this could not have been a conscious thought.

The shade of green was beautiful, but I still asked if I could have clean sheets. I was told that the sheets were changed only once a week and that it was too soon.

People arrived to visit, crew members of other airlines and, of course, my own. My supervisor, Doris, arrived from Dallas. Other visitors arrived. Word was out in the hotel grapevine that an American Airlines flight attendant was in the Red Cross hospital.

"Oh, yes," they would say, "her appendix was very slowly rupturing as the captain started descent into Narita."

"She didn't know, of course, just thought she was jet lagged."

"Of course," the sympathetic listeners nodded. "Jet lag. Awake for twenty-four hours or more."

American Airlines was once again very good to me and put my sister, Brenda, into the same hotel where the layover crew stayed, The Tokyu Inn. Next would come my supervisor, Doris.

Brenda came at the same time as my supervisor who was in the room. Brenda stated that some folks from another airline gave her liquor miniatures, which she brought to give to me. I almost started crying as the one thing we could never do is pilfer from our aircrafts, especially liquor!

I begged my sister for a drink of water, which the staff would not give me, as that was not in their instructions. Brenda wouldn't either!

By then, I'd had enough, so I got out of bed and informed all that I was going to the American Embassy and catching a flight right out of Japan. "Yes, right out of here! I am serious. I mean it," I said as I fell back into bed.

One night I called in a nurse and said, "I am in so much pain."

She turned and walked out of the room, and I could hear her say, "I'm in pain, I'm in pain," in a sing-song voice as she walked in the corridor. I don't remember if she helped me or not, but most likely she did.

The next day, she came in and brought a picture album of her plays in which she had performed in a kabuki theater! How kind! Perhaps she was not annoyed with me. I acted pleased for her to share with me. And I was.

This very same nurse asked if she could help me with washing my hair, over the trough above the many urine-filled, multi-gallon jugs, of pregnant women, in this same ward.

When you have been in a hospital in a foreign country, delirious from feeling like shards of glass are racing through your body, kindnesses are the healing breath of God.

Once, a team of Japanese doctors came into my room. They stood in a circle above me, looking down. When doctors examine a patient, they place a towel over the incision and then gently lift it up, to be respectful of one's modesty, I suppose. They all took a turn tsk-tsking at the sight of my long vertical incision.

Then they asked me if I liked Japan.

"I love Japan!" I replied.

Life Is a Stamp Collection

Looking down at me with beautiful identical Asian eyes, they smiled in unison.

The evening before, my new interpreter friend, Reiko, was to have her surgery, I slid a note under the door wishing her well. This is a layover custom amongst flight crews to not awaken a potential guest!

Later that day, her husband sat out in the corridor across from my room. He spoke to me when I emerged, and he introduced himself. He expressed how kind it was of me to leave a note for Reiko, his wife. He said that she was doing well.

Sometime later, my brother, Roger, and I flew back to Narita, Japan to reunite with the nurse who spoke English and had interpreted for me from the moment I was wheeled through the hospital doors. She was invaluable, and we wanted to thank her on the family's behalf. So, after we arrived at the Red Cross hospital, Roger stood straight and bowed toward her as is the Japanese custom of respect. She noticed.

I took a bag of towels that had been loaned to me during my stay. Japanese workers had found a pair of men's pajamas and some rubber thongs when I was wheeled in and admitted to a room. Ordinarily, a patient's relatives would bring the necessities for the patient's stay.

Also in the hospital was an American Airlines flight attendant who had had an accident while out jogging in the farm fields behind our hotel. I was visited by a corporate American Airlines doctor who was to accompany the injured girl back to DFW. He explained that they would be returning on an American Airlines flight to DFW. "Why not a corporate jet instead of a 777?" I asked. He explained that the corporate jet is much lighter, and one of our jumbo jets would be more stable in rough air. Of course.

When some of the flight crews for other airlines heard about me, they were very compassionate with my sister and sent messages to me through her. Crew members knew what it was like to have an unexpected illness during a work trip, though illnesses the extent of mine were rare. One of the emotions that connects all crew members is that our identification with the seriousness of our responsibilities toward our passengers and fellow crew members. A kinship forms, no matter what the name of the airline.

Everyone asked if there was anything they could do. Just say a prayer. Buddhist or Christian. I believe it all goes to the same place.

Many months earlier, I was on a layover in Narita, and as usual, a group decided to take the hotel bus into the center of town and have a dinner and some relaxation.

Several times we stopped into a small store and bought a can of *saki* which had a long pin with it which was for inserting in a location which would trigger heat for making the *saki* hot. One night on the way to the bus, Pam and I stopped and bought a can for the bus ride back to the Tokyu Hotel.

We took seats all the way in the back, which were elevated, and we could see forward as we imbibed our small *saki* drinks. Arriving at our location, we were now ready for a second sleep before flying home to our base the following morning.

Frank, a mechanic, was a US citizen and an aircraft mechanic for another US airline as he was based in Narita. He was married to a Japanese woman. She never came out with him, as Japanese women seem to stay at home with the children in the evening. Basically, Frank was a "crew bum." I suppose any layover crew was entertainment for him.

One night out in Narita, most of the crew went back to the Tokyu Hotel in its bus. However, Frank had too much to drink, and so Pam decided to drive his car with *right hand drive*, and on the opposite side of the street on which we drive in the States. Unfortunately, she hit a Japanese man who was riding his bicycle home from his job as a bar tender at that hour. They did not stop to render aid.

Not knowing about Pam's incident, the next morning, many of the crew members along with the captain chartered a bus to take them to Mt. Fuji for a "climb." During this drive, the bus was called and told that one of their crewmembers had been arrested and shackled in the lobby of the layover hotel. The captain had the bus turn around, not realizing what had transpired, I'm sure.

After spending some time in the Narita Jail, Pam was tried by a group of Japanese judges, unlike the States where we are tried by a jury of our peers. She was sentenced to a prison term in Chiba Prefecture.

Several of the crew on layovers went by train to visit Pam in prison. I did not know her well, only to work with and to drink *saki* in the back seat of our hotel bus while returning to the Tokyu Inn. Prison and saki. This was something new to experience and to see another side of Japanese society.

Our train travelled through snow down to the coast of the Pacific Ocean. We then traveled to Chiba Prison by taxi, as I remember. When we arrived at the grounds of the prison, we waited out in a small building with a stove heating for warmth. I noticed a man with part of his small finger severed, waiting there as well. Later I was told that a severed little finger indicated loyalty to the *yakuza,* an underground Mafia group, who kept order in the streets of Japan by extracting "protection sums" from the shopkeepers. This rendered very little crime on Japan's city streets.

Finally, our crew group was allowed into the prison meeting area for Pam. A sumo wrestler-type man in navy uniform sat with Pam on one side of a glass partition. We sat on the other side. The guard took notes of our conversation and chuckled when we made a funny comment.

We exchanged greetings with Pam, who looked fine. She said that they watched everything that she did. She said that for exercise she walked constantly in her cell. The "powers that be" admonished her and told her to sit and meditate more.

As she had a window in her cell, she could see the snow below. She said she envisioned lying on top of the snow and making snow angels.

She had to clean her own food bowl of the congealed egg and rice breakfast dish. She commented that clean as she might, it never got totally removed. "Clean as she might …" There was only cold water.

Then one of the flight attendants who had been in touch with a publishing company, gave Pam some information about "writing after prison about her experiences." I don't believe this ever came about.

We had the transcript for Pam's trial which was witnessed by judges in Japan. On the train ride back to Narita, we went over the notes. As we read the transcript, it was most interesting. Pam said that she did not realize she had killed someone. One of the judges disputed that, commenting that she knew she had hit someone but chose not to stop.

After the train ride while waiting for the hotel bus in Narita, which is very near a McDonald's, we ducked in there to get something warm to drink. Frank was there, and Sally went over to him and said we were returning from Chiba after seeing Pam. He said, without emotion, "I know, I know." I wondered if his wife even knew about this death. I wondered if he ever stopped drinking and quit being a crew bum. Well, not my life, but I do feel compassion for all this. Except for Frank.

American Airlines paid quite a hefty sum to the dead man's family, as I understand it.

Chapter Seventeen

At Home on Marco Island

During the frightening experience in Japan of peritonitis and ruptured appendix, I made a decision that if I were to survive, I would return to Marco Island, Florida, and begin living my dreams. I would find a way to build a home on my vacant lot situated on a beautiful little bay and canal. I set about building my new house. That home was indeed completed, and my sister helped me move in during July 2001. I had purchased plants for indoors and had put the final touches to the interior. Then, I left to work a flight from Dallas to Osaka, Japan on September 10, 2001. I had not yet retired from American Airlines.

The Terrifying 9/11 Disaster

With the international date change, we arrived in Osaka on September 11, 2001. At midnight that night—it was now September 12th in Osaka, but still September 11th in the US—I awoke and turned on the television to International CNN. The news of 9/11 was frightening, terrifying. The entire world was stunned. I thought I was watching a horror movie.

To this day, I cherish the kindness of people from many countries who helped our fellow American Airlines crews and passengers. I was so fortunate to be in a hotel that showed extreme kindness to our crew. The hotel management sent a small vase of lovely flowers to each crew member's room with a note of condolence for our loss of fellow crew members in New York and Washington.

I did not get scheduled to go back to my home in the States for two weeks.

Meanwhile, American Airlines, as usual, was very good to us crew members. Routinely, our Captain checked on us at least once each day. And the airline authorized us to make two calls a day to our home country. That generous gesture gave us a much-needed connection during this time of stress.

We all agreed to convene in our crew room on the sixth floor of our hotel at 1500 hours. Crews of several different flights were there. Most of the American Airlines crew members had been onboard an aircraft for many hours and had limited personal items and clothing. Now, with an indefinite stay ahead of us, we needed to augment our supplies.

We found a Gap outlet near our hotel. I found that if I shopped in the men's section for slacks, they would be about the right length for my height.

We soon made friends with a UPS crew, who were also staying at our hotel on the Osaka Bay. We were told that some of the filming for the *Titanic* took place at this hotel. The UPS crew told us that they had been in place in the cockpit of their 747 cargo plane with the door shut, ready to release the brakes for their outbound flight to Hong Kong when a call came from the tower: "Turn off engines. There is a problem in New York with some buildings. Your flight is cancelled!"

The UPS crew said they had received a briefing before they left the States anticipating "perhaps an impending situation." Our American Airlines captain said he had not been given a briefing before his last departure.

For the next few days, we all waited for word to come from the US crew-scheduling departments of our respective airlines. We waited. We continued to wait. We so appreciated each other's presence and support as we waited for word. When one is in a foreign country and your native land has shown such vulnerability and you are far away from all that anchors you, well, it is definitely a growth experience.

The Japanese hotel guests and staff showed us extraordinary courtesy and consideration. If we entered an elevator, the Japanese would ask us if we were Americans. As we answered, "Yes," they would back away from us and not enter the same car. At first, I thought perhaps because our airline had been involved two times in the 9/11 deaths that they did not want to be around us. However, I soon learned that when there has been death as in this case of our coworkers, fellow countrymen, the Japanese show respect and give kindness and space, so as not to intrude. I will forever be grateful for their kindness and consideration as fellow world citizens.

I certainly cannot fault anyone over my being employed for forty years and then being a retiree from a bankrupt airline. It was just where I was supposed to be, a walkin' across oceans type of person, answering questions like, "What time do we land in Frankfurt?"

"Oh, 7:00 a.m."

"Is that the time in Dallas?"

"No, there is only one landing time in Frankfurt, and it's the one for their time zone."

"Oh."

I tried several times to go in another direction, but it just would never materialize for any length of time. Heavens, I became engaged three times thinking, *Now I will quit.*

But the job always lasted longer than the interest in getting married.

Philosophers' Café

A few years after I moved into my house on Marco Island, I started a discussion group called "The Marco Island Philosophers' Café." This was a group of twelve to fifteen people who met at my house once each month to discuss a particular topic or classic book. It was a most enjoyable experience. Following are a few examples of the types of subjects:

On a Friday in early December 2005, my brother Roger was our guest and "Presenter of Interest."

On a Sunday that same month, we met at Juan Munera's Gallery Studio for a talk and discussion on art and philosophy, and touched on the manipulation of society and religion through art.

On a Sunday in January 2006, Lubomira Samantha Sheehy was our Presenter of Interest. The topic was her life as a young Polish girl under German Occupation. She had been taken at the age of twelve from her home in Poland and put on a train to Germany to be a nanny in an SS officer's home.

One day when the war had ended, the officer came home and told her to "Get out, get out. the war is over." She took her few things and went out to the road in front of his house. Another nanny was walking there, and the two of them joined up. Soon a flatbed truck with American GIs came along and gave them a ride into the nearby town. Lubomira never saw any of her family again.

She stated that she contacted the Red Cross to help locate her family, and they said to her, and I quote, "Don't you know how busy we are?"

She somehow got to England where she studied and became a nurse. She ended up in Detroit and then later moved to Chicago. There she met and married Charlie Sheehy, her future American husband. One thing he said to her was that he was not so sure he wanted children, and she said to me, that she told Charlie it was fine with her.

Lubomira was a very talented artist. On their house interior walls on Marco Island, many beautiful pictures hung that were from their travels. Since she herself was an artist, she painted in her upper studio, looking out over a beautiful Marco Island canal. There she painted a lovely floral painting with a lot of black background which she gave to me.

I am delighted to have it as Lubomira has died. Hopefully she and her American Charlie can rest together away from the memories of German invasion, war, and abandonment.

Another couple contributed much to our conversations, Rodrigue and Carole Tremblay, from Vaudreuil, Quebec.

Rodrigue served as Minister of Industry and Trade in the Canadian government. Ridrigue (Tremblay) has written many scores of books used around the world in Universities. One of his works is, *The Code of Global Ethics: Ten Humanist Principles*. On the front cover is a picture of a crystal engraved ball of the world, which I gave to those who had been a presenter more than twice, of topics in our Marco Island Philospher's Group held in my home.

His wife, Carole Jean Tremblay wrote a fantastic novel called *CyberCash*. Among her many literary credits are several delightful children's books as well as written a few scores of books on economics. Many are used in foreign universities as textbooks. Both Rodrigue and Carole are inquisitive about all aspects of life, and this serves them well, as they give lectures onboard cruise ships, occasionally and in our local "Naples Renaissance Academy." They met at the University of California in Stanford, California.

Now, this would not be complete if I did not mention a wonderful couple, Karol and Ryszarda (Lida) Pelc. They are from Poland, and live now part time in the Upper Peninsula of Michigan and part time on Marco Island, Fl. The Pelcs traveled quite often to foreign destinations with the Fulbright Foundation. They live in Michigan in the summer generally, and the rest of the year, they are in Florida. When friends asked Karol about Ryszarda, his wife, he smiled and said he told them "Oh, she is sitting on the beach in Florida writing poetry, while I am here in Michigan." Laughter would ensue.

Ryszarda is a very accomplished poetess. I have asked her permission to put down one of her poems. So, please enjoy the freshness of her thoughts.

"Islander's Confession" by Rysarda (Lida) Pelc

I have to confess my sins.
I am guilty of doing nothing
except walking on the beach crushing under my feet,
dazzling in sun ray, shiny fragile shells.

I have to confess my guilt of doing nothing
but watching dignified white egrets;
> survivors of evolution, brown pelicans;
> clattery, puffy, arrogant beggars, sea gulls;
> skimmers and tiny, hasty, amusing sandpipers.

I'm guilty. I do nothing but admire the flying birds
under azure sky,above the emerald mirror of
shimmering waters.
I'm guilty of waiting for dolphins, hoping to watch
them while they chase a school of fish, when they play
in deep waters of the Gulf, while they jump high and
their dark bodies reflect the sunbeams.

I confess; I spend hours sitting on the beach, I spend
hours seated on the beach
sifting the white, fine sand through my fingers,
listening to the soothing sound of waves, - reminder of
a long forgotten sound of water as listening to, while
floating safely in my mother's womb - before I was
born.

Karol Pelc, the husband of this interesting and talented duo, had an article published called "Surviving the Holocaust," printed in the Michigan Tech newsletter of approximately September 1, 2000. This interview is from Karol's office of Business and Economics, in which he taught. He has given me permission to take from it anything I want, as his family was separated by the Germans when he was quite young.

In one paragraph, and there are many descriptive ones in this article, Karol describes how he, at the age of nine, left home very early to walk a one-mile route to the church in the dark to serve as an altar boy. He met the German patrol in the same place, every day. He knew they were a foreign force and were killing his people.

One day when Karol was returning home from his secret underground school, he was stopped by the German police and forced to go down another street. There, the soldiers were pushing people to a place of execution while assembling a crowd to watch.

"Twenty men were standing along a wall," Karol states. Because he was small, the Germans put him in front of the crowd so he could see. From ten feet away, he watched the men being shot. It was terrible with the bodies falling. He was scared to death. Karol had to watch, or he would have been shot too. "That's the terror that comes from physical domination."

My comment is that these Poles had so much courage. And any writing that describes these horrors must be an understatement.

On the TV one evening was a program by the BBC about the Katyn Forest massacre. I had not heard about this forest or of any massacre. This forest is on the western edge of Russia, and Stalin was in power when this occurred in 1940. The program led one to believe a question still remains as to whether the Germans or the Soviets had done the murdering because the wire around the wrists of the men was made in Germany. Were the executing bullets as well, or were they manufactured by the Russians?

I was told later by Karol, that it was the Russian manufacturing of both that had been proven; 22,000 Polish Jews and non-Jews, the learned, educated class of Poland, were executed and put into a pit.

Karol told me that one should not say *Nazis*, but *Germans*, as giving the perpetrators a name other than that, allows the Germans to feel excused. Karol's father was executed at Katyn Forest. Poland had more non-Jews executed than any other nation. On a sad side note, Karol Pelc died unexpectedly on August 26, 2020, with their only son, Darius, preceding him in death, about eleven months earlier.

On a Sunday in February 2006, Andrew Kazczak was the Presenter of Interest. The topic: Evolutionary Humanism.

Andrew Kazcak was another fascinating addition to our Group. He had been awarded "The Silver Cross Jubilee" by Queen Elizabeth for his work in the Polish underground during

World War Two. He had worked with Karol Wojtyla (Pope John Paul II) in the Polish underground movement, trying to defeat the Germans who had invaded their country.

He and Karol were acquaintances. They knew who each other was, and they were working for one common purpose, again to defeat the Germans.

He met and married a lovely English lady, Elizabeth Robinson, and they immigrated to Canada.

Elizabeth told the story of Andrew calling and asking her out. When she went to the door expecting to see him, he was standing across the street under an umbrella, holding a bouquet of flowers, in the rain with streetlights in the background.

That was when she knew they would be together for their life's next adventures.

We were not a book club, but we did discuss *The Rise and Fall of Civilizations*. Another book that discussed the philosophy of groups and their decisions was Jared Diamond's book, *Collapse*. We talked about this one as well. This was especially interesting to me because Diamond writes about the clear-cutting of forests and indicates that while the cutters made contracts to replant book after the cutting, they skipped out with the money and never replanted. This happened in lowland forests of the Malay Peninsula, then Borneo, then the Solomon Islands and Sumatra, now the Philippines and, coming up soon, New Guinea, the Amazon, and the Congo Basin. As he says in his book, "What was the guy thinking who cut down the last tree on Easter Island?"

The Forester My Father Trusted

Jared Diamond's stories reminded me of the forester Daddy had trusted in the 1950s while he was in the Foreign Service. It was not until I took over the running Daddy's timber tracts, including supervising the selective cutting of trees, did I realize that this man had stolen millions. At the very end, he clear-cut and never replanted. One of our tracts which had been clear-cut was surrounded by the National Forest of Arkansas.

I walked on the tracts, and we rode Honda 3-wheelers on these rattle-snake-infested lands in Texas. My brother was with me and a man with a gun, in case we came upon a truck and men with cutting saws stealing the trees on Daddy's properties in Arkansas and Texas.

In the end, the forester, a "nice man" named J.D. Crownover, was our rattlesnake.

While my brother was embroiled in a lawsuit against him on our family's behalf, the SOB died. And I don't mean *sahib*.

I don't really understand why some people are so overtly dismissive of other's rights and property. Where is the world's conscience, individually and collectively? Where is an individual man's heart, logic, and charity?

We see that our Congress members are allowed to take donations/bribes called as a "lobbying" mechanism. Many deeds are definitely influencing toward the Congress.

Hypocrisy.

Well, let me tell you about the kind of hypocrisy many people have observed. In 1966, my brother Roger entered Baylor Law School. There he met a very smart and beautiful girl from Plainview, Texas, Cynthia Smith.

Many years later, Ken Starr was appointed President of Baylor. He was let go after the following:

He, who was so previously challenging toward President Clinton, chose to overlook terrible behavior by members of the Baylor football team, including their rapes. This was detailed in the papers. Even Baylor's Board seemed to hide inside the sands of their Bibles and to think women were not worthy of decent human behavior.

Recently, Ken Starr was on *Fox News,* being quite eloquent in his advice on some subject.

Really, are there simply no standards anymore, Ken Starr, to which you will not sink to? Asking for a friend ...

M. Angela Sanders

Guardian Ad Litem Volunteer

In mid-2006, I joined Guardian Ad Litem as a volunteer and was assigned my first child. The nineteen-month-old girl lived in the Everglades area of Florida, in Port of the Islands. When I went to visit the child, the mosquitoes ate me for dinner. The father and the child were not at home. The mom, who was on drugs and crack the whole time during the pregnancy, had deserted the baby. The father had a police record. I was scared he might be mean, but this is something I had volunteered to do, and I was sure it would turn out all right. You know, if I can survive a ride in a Jeep at night with a leopard jumping on the hood as we return from the cinema in the Himalayas, what is a little old visit with a police-record dad?

Six months later, I went to court for the first time on a case connected with my Guardian Ad Litem volunteering. It was a case in which the Collier Court System for abused, abandoned, and neglected children was returning a child whom I had been keeping an eye on here on Marco Island to her very pregnant parent. What a deal. The mother gave birth to the baby while she was incarcerated in Alabama for grand larceny. The father was a drug dealer and had landed in jail in Florida. The girl of twenty-two months, who had been staying with her grandmother, was now going back to her reunited parents. Yes, the child indeed was returned to her parents. There are not always so many choices, but the courts did try very hard, I saw.

So many things are being done the best way we know how, and we may not always get it right, but staff and volunteers have their hearts in the highest place. The volunteers' wisdom and dedication are an example for us all.

For instance, one couple donated mattresses to homes that provided shelter to a child being removed from a family home, whether during an emergency situation or not. If a family ended up in the local abuse safe house or shelter, the whole family was placed in one room. Kitchen space was given for each family.

When a family must leave quickly, there is not always time for clothing, etc. If the escaping family has a car in which to arrive at the abuse shelter, there is often a place to park the car so it cannot be seen from the roads.

A group of ladies make quilts. Then each child is given a newly-made quilt to sleep under each night while there. This 'comfort' quilt went with the children when it was time for them to leave, hopefully in safety. Sometimes they were given a cell phone, refurbished ones, which many donated.

We donated money for the family so they could get a new apartment in the local area. The money was for purchasing towels, silverware, in our thrift shop, "Options."

In one case, the offending spouse did find the family again. One child dialed 911 and threw the phone under a bed. The call went through, and the police were dispatched. The police arrived, but sadly they were too late.

It takes much emotional wisdom and energy of the male and female volunteers, for sure. I was there for only a few short years as burnout happened to me.

One of the men volunteers told a story about a little black boy. Ivan had a rough beginning in life. He was now in the court system and was adopted by a white couple, who were overjoyed to have him, to make their family complete! He was home!

Then, this couple became pregnant. They said that they could no longer see their family with Ivan in it. This male volunteer went to pick up Ivan, and he was extremely angry. As a little child, would we not all be? What could the man say, after he had previously reassured Ivan he had a permanent and forever home?

Of course, that was then, but now is now .... I often wondered how the story ended.

Chapter Eighteen

Back to India after 60 years.

In 2012, sixty years from when we had landed on the subcontinent of India in 1952, my three siblings and I took a reunion trip to India!

Craig, Angela, Brenda, Roger

Life Is a Stamp Collection

It was a tremendous trip, as we were going to visit Rajasthan, where I had never been. As we circled over the Indira Gandhi airport, I wondered what it would be like to be with my brothers and sister, as adults, and review our former homeland. We landed in New Delhi, after many hours of flight from DFW and Dubai. We stayed in a Marriott, and I was a little shocked to see beef on the menu. Sacred cows are part of the Hindu religion!

As we walked inside the beautiful marble Indira Gandhi terminal to baggage claim, it was modern and beautiful, and it felt so "right." I could smell the cooking/heating fuel of cow dung patty fumes wafting inside this lovely, marbled hall.

Yes, indeed we were back into our old childhood rhythm, and this time we would be visiting Rajasthan, a romantic place of lore.

Rajas, elephants with handsome coverings, beautiful bright fabrics, would be our delight. A *mahout* is an elephant trainer and caretaker. Their relationship starts early in both their lives. The *mahout* rides behind the elephant's ears. The *mahout* changes direction using his feet.

Rajasthan, with small canals for irrigation, was very lush in comparison to much of India. The crops were large and healthy, lined up in neat rows as in more-developed countries.

The Maharaja was quite young, seventeen, and he was away in boarding school in India. His mother oversaw the daily government affairs while he was gone.

His palaces were beautiful and carved ever so artfully. One was white and sat in the middle of a lake, surrounded by water.

A beggar woman mindlessly swept dirt over rocks next to the road. Over and over and over. Another woman, ever-so-skinny, held a baby. She looked at us and made the gesture of putting her hand down to the baby and then up to her mouth.

The government of India asked that no one give to beggars as it keeps the person in a certain depressed state of self-growth and respect. We can all understand that logic, but this baby and its mother were no doubt seriously hungry.

Here we all rode elephants, two each on the elephants, to a palace of interest. There is always a story around the occupants who built the palace. The royalty who lived in the palace, the Maharaja, and his friends sat outdoors and played chess with the beautiful girls being the chess pieces. They moved them around the different marble squares in order to achieve Checkmate.

Our trip was a reunion trip for us, but the one place was had not been to was Rajastan. Above is some of the history of how the royalty lived in that State. It was therefore new to us in our second home country, as we had never been there previously.

Then we returned to Delhi which had been a location where previously we had a family home. My friend, Rana Jaaj, from many years ago, came to our hotel and visited with us. She invited me to go to the Gymkhana Club for lunch, while the others went on a bit of a tour, in Old and New Delhi.

I had never been to a Gymkhana club which was for the British in the days of Empire Rule. I loved the idea that, now, I would have this experience. It also seems that the membership is passed down from one generation to the next generation.

While we were there, Rana met a notorious *rani sahib*. This woman walked around with a young Caucasian man who was, ostensibly, her helper. How nice to meet with Indian royalty, if you can call it that. There is so much about India that is unique to its people and country. I love it.

A Gymkhana club is where gentlemen meet to play snooker, have smokes, and drink G and Ts under swaying wide fans. These fans are powered by servants pulling on ropes.

In the olden days, the Gymkhana was where they discussed the latest news from all around the world, such as "I say, did you hear about the Raja of Jaipur and his bout of measles?" or "Did you hear that the East India Company is now exporting maize?" and such and such.

As our road trip to Rajasthan had been over a serious washboard road with constant tiny bumps, one of my brothers bought us air tickets back to Delhi to connect to our Dubai-based airline, for our trip to Dubai where we spent a few days.

Goodbye to American Airlines

I retired as an American Airlines International flight attendant after completing forty years and managing post 9-11 flying. I will always be grateful that American Airlines hired me in 1963! It was my second interview!

Chapter Nineteen

A Day on Capitol Hill with Senator Bill and Grace Nelson

At a Naples social club to which I belonged, there was a raffle for bidding to win a day "On Capitol Hill with Senator Bill Nelson." I did not know his political affiliation, and I saw that only one person had bid, so I put down a bid a bit higher than hers. The raffle benefited The Abuse Shelter of Naples, Florida.

I bid, and I won!

The Nelsons were most gracious and went out of their way to familiarize me with the Dirkson Building and the Capital. Grace Nelson took me to the Senate dining room where I saw Hillary Clinton, Jean Kirkpatrick, and other notables.

This was memorable to me, and I thank the Nelsons again for their time. But what was special as I look back on that event was the fact that Senator Bill Nelson had been an astronaut on the Columbia.

A little history of the race to space. Construction began on the spaceship Columbia in 1975 while I was living in Southern California. I did not realize until sometime later the significance of this for the space program. On January 12, 1986, the first sitting member of the House of Representatives, Bill Nelson, went into space on the Shuttle Columbia. He had won the election for the 47th District, South Florida. His title on the shuttle Columbia STS-61-C was Payload Specialist. This was January 12-18, 1986. Later, Bill Nelson was elected as a Florida Senator and would serve beginning in 2001.

On February 1, 2003, I was on a layover in Narita, Japan, and had CNN on the TV. They came on and said that the shuttle was overdue for its return. It was time for me to go downstairs and walk on the treadmill. When I entered the gym, most of the people were not watching CNN. I asked if they would mind if we turned the TV to a news channel. I said the shuttle was overdue and had not returned. At this, some people left. I had hoped this news was dubious, but, as it turned out, it was real.

On January 16, 2003, the Columbia spacecraft blasted off from Cape Kennedy, with seven astronauts. Kalpana Chawla, born in Karmel, India, was the Payload Specialist on this mission. She was also the very first Indian woman into space.

The Columbia was on its 27th mission when it disintegrated upon reentry. Its debris fell on Texas and Louisiana. Some remains were found, however most of the remains became particles in space. The records state that some of Kalpana Chawla's remains were found and were sent to India for a Hindu ceremony.

Whenever I hear of an outstanding accomplishment of an Indian, I feel pride for my second-home nation of the 1950s. So, as India continues their evolving multi-subjects' pace of the worlds' largest democracy, I am proud of them.

"Welcome to Florida" Women's International Club

Marian Adair established "Welcome Clubs International" in 1959 for returning wives from the US Foreign Service. Her first club was in Washington, DC. She felt that when families return, they have been out of step with normal, day to day American life. Here, returning wives would become a little more in sync with ladies of similar experiences as theirs. I enjoyed being a part of that club, but I was also still working as a flight attendant. Once I forgot to pay my club dues, and I was bounced out of the club. Later Marian took me by the hand and walked me over to the Treasurer and humorously said, "Could you make sure this child pays her dues next year?" She had a fun sense of humor.

Because they wintered in Naples, Fla., Marian and other ladies began a "Welcome to Florida" club. I had retired and living on Marco Island. I heard about this club for foreign-born ladies who were trying to become more familiar with our country and its customs. I thought how much I would enjoy that, but I was born in Searcy, Arkansas. And so that was that.

My friend, Christine, now living on Marco Island after being divorced from a Swedish man, asked if I would be interested in joining. I said that I did not meet the requirements. It seems that later the requirements were changed, and I was eligible to join. This was around 1993! I suppose they counted me an "International."

By now I had met a tremendous couple from Lickskillet, Indiana, Leon and Florence Hesser. I asked Florence if she would like to join. Florence had been a wife and mother in Islamabad, Pakistan, and later in East Pakistan (Bangladesh). She had several honors as well, such as setting up a Learning Center in Saudi Arabia, upon request of the Saudi Royal Family.

Let me tell you about one of the interesting ladies in our "Welcome to Florida Club." Nancy Furstner was born in Scotland and immigrated to the US as a four-year-old, I believe. She was the perfect lady to be invited into "Welcome to Florida." When we had International Day, she would walk in the small indoor parade dressed in her lovely Scottish clan kilt.

One Christmas, she e-mailed me that her husband had had a bad health diagnosis, and she was saying it would be a sad holiday. A few days after Christmas, Earnest died unexpectedly. He was an exceptional man, raised in Germany, where he had been a soldier in Hitler's Youth Army. After he and Nancy met here in the States, they married and lived in various places where he designed, planned, and oversaw the installation of kitchens in international hotels around the world. He was also an avid runner and underwater photographer. He had marvelous photographic shows around Naples. These were only a few of his experiences and talents.

Rummikub

    A mutual friend, Polly, suggested to me that we get four ladies and play Rummikub together to get Nancy back to being a little happier.

    We all soon had a very close and kind friendship. A French lady, Florence, joined us well. Being with the United Nations for thirty years, she had an interesting background, having been stationed from Paris to New York.

    This grew to be a pleasant occasion each month as for sure lunch was included as well by those three who could cook beautifully. I made luncheon reservations.

Epilogue: Reflections

As I reflect on my most memorable experiences, what or where do I begin?

When I was ten-years-old, the first time I saw the Taj Mahal, I was enthralled by the exquisite beauty. It was built by Shah Jahan as homage to his wife, Mumtaj Mahal, who died in childbirth with their thirteenth child.

In 1978, when I moved with my American Eskimo dog, Sacha, to Punta Bandera, Baja, Mexico, I could not imagine how blessed I was. When something is right to do, it truly is like a wind to your back. I watched the whales from the Pacific migrating to San Ignacio Lagoon in southern Baja to bear their young. At night I fell asleep to the sounds of the Pacific waves crashing under the cliff. Sometimes I could see an American helicopter with a blinking red light checking out large ships going to our west coast. These ships represented freedoms and choices for Americans and our enterprise systems.

Choice is also a factor Americans have that citizens of many other countries do not have.

This is the way life should be, free to go where your heart leads and wants. I think I have learned that there will never be enough times for my intense curiosity. I find that my diverse learning about a subject is not quenched until I have visited the location and experienced the depth of delight/sorrow/deep/spiritual joy/humility.

In 1979, in Peru, the children would come out of stilt shacks and stare at us, probably because of our coloring and the way we were dressed.

Life Is a Stamp Collection

In Kenya, Africa, sleeping in a tent, we could hear the elephants roar, which sounded like lions.

I remember the times I have looked out the window at the moonlight as a flight attendant, seeing the moon sitting on a cloud, during my required rest break at 35,000 feet.

In Paris on the third Thursday in November, as a celebration of a new wine, Beaujolais Nouveau, is rushed to the airports for the first shipment out. The locals would paint their faces and celebrate in the streets.

The Christmas Festival in Mainz, near Frankfurt, Germany, was festive. I walked around with hot wine to keep me warm.

I was told that one should always ask God for wisdom with discernment. I pray that our President Biden and leaders of other countries of the world choose wisdom with discernment!

Everything that happens in our world is right on schedule. Our reactions are our responsibility. We must make them appropriate and carefully analyzed. As we know we must watch our words as words can hurt others, in their hearts. That pain never heals but does strengthen us.

Children, the environment, and pets are the recipients of our lack of correct thought. The world is not here just for us to put smog into Los Angeles and New Delhi.

We owe China, Iraq, Iran, Polynesia, and others for their art and accomplishments from many, many years ago which furthered us as humans and our societies.

Two people who were special to me that were mentioned in the book are Karol Pelc, who passed during the writing of this book over the past two years, and Rana Sundar Singh. Rana married Gurdip Singh. Their friendships are everlasting.

One final tidbit …

One December, I think, a group of flight attendants from the LAX base went to the AA Learning center in Ft. Worth, Texas to be trained on the new 747. We were so excited to learn about it! This would open new opportunities for new destinations, and this was tremendous!

One of the first trips I worked was to Dulles Field Virginia near (Washington DC) from LAX. It really was a thrill to land there and be met by six black luxury limousines. We each had a lot of space, needless to say, as for eighteen total crew members, the math worked out to only three attendants per limo.

As we were driven past the giant 747, in a parade line of luxury cars, exiting the tarmac, it was a wonderful experience for this little Arkansas girl, who had grown up, riding in rickshaws and on elephant backs.

This now, was truly the ride of the Maharajas.

Rana Sundar Singh and Gurdip Singh
Wedding photo

www.ingramcontent.com/pod-product-compliance
Lightning Source LLC
Chambersburg PA
CBHW071833080526
44589CB00012B/1003